Letters and papers. With a memoir by Harry Graham

Algernon Hyde Villiers

LETTERS AND PAPERS OF ALGERNON HYDE VILLIERS

LETTERS AND PAPERS OF ALGERNON HYDE VILLIERS

WITH A MEMOIR BY
HARRY GRAHAM

Man with his burning soul
Has but an hour of breath
To build a ship of truth
In which his soul may sail—
Sail on the sea of death,
For death takes toll
Of beauty, courage, youth,
Of all but truth. . . .

J. MASEFIELD

LONDON
SOCIETY FOR PROMOTING
CHRISTIAN KNOWLEDGE
NEW YORK: THE MACMILLAN COMPANY
1919

A. H. V.

(February 1st, 1886—November 23rd, 1917)

"HIS brother-officers could not speak too highly of his capacity as a leader, of his charm as a companion, and of all those splendid qualities of his which made him the leading spirit of his mess and the idol of his men. He loved his men, and they loved him, and his invincible optimism carried him safely through those dark hours of danger and discomfort which set weaker men grumbling and despairing. It is no exaggeration to say that officers and men adored him.

No one more willingly gave up a life of noble promise to a call which he felt was sacred. He thought that in the war there was an inspiration to call men from 'poverty of outlook' (his own expression), and to direct all their energies into the maintenance of a supremely righteous cause.

With all his radiant enjoyment of this world, and his artistic temperament, which found fit expression in a lovely voice, as well as in painting and spirited writing, full of ease, force, and grace, the vision of the highest never left him. The spiritual element in his nature was far the strongest, and the life of Christ was always before him as the one great example.

He was happy in the circumstances of his death. For he had a peculiar love of France, and the spirit of comradeship in the Army realised his ideal of the brotherhood of man, as a life of sacrifice and adventure appealed to the truest instincts of his being."—*The Times*, December 8th, 1917.

CONTENTS

vii

LETTERS AND PAPERS OF ALGERNON HYDE VILLIERS

I

MEMOIR

" I WISH I had time," Algernon Villiers wrote in one of his last letters, " to arrange my theologico-seraphic fancies into a series of papers. I should like to straighten them all out into a consecutive view of the whole great subject. Perhaps, however, this will come later and will be better worth doing with further knowledge."

This project he was not spared to carry through, but in place of that " consecutive view " it has been thought well to publish fragments from his correspondence, dealing for the most part with spiritual matters—the broken arc, as it were, which he was never able to weld together into a perfect round.

The selection of private letters for publication, after the death of the writer, is always a difficult and delicate task, involving questions of discretion upon which perhaps no two persons will be agreed. So much that is purely personal must be eliminated from such letters, that a perusal of what is left may tempt the reader to reach entirely false conclusions. I cannot indeed help feeling that in an age when to be seriously absorbed in the only things that really matter is still looked upon as a mark of slight eccentricity, the extracts included in this volume may give the impression that Algernon Villiers' interest in the study of religious and spiritual questions was something abnormal. That this was ever the case must appear impossible to any one who knew him at all; the absurdity of such an idea would be patent to his most casual acquaintance. There never was a man more healthy in mind or body, nor one who better loved the simple joys of life—laughter and song, sunshine and beauty. None showed a keener appreciation of a joke, or entered with a more infectious gaiety into all mundane pleasures and interests. Music gave him the intense delight which comes from an artistic imagination, and his tuneful tenor voice and powers of expression brought to his singing an especial charm. He was unusually sensitive to every kind of beauty, and the little water-colour sketches which he was so fond of making show him to have possessed a fine sense of colour and form. As a friend of early days said of him, he wore his religion lightly in the ordinary intercourse of life.

There was nothing on the surface of his character to suggest that he was conscious of a message or interested in any world but this. To the casual acquaintance and even to some of his close friends he appeared simply the embodiment of high-minded common sense. He had a rare facility in combining industry with enjoyment, and seemed endowed with all the qualities which make for worldly popularity, prosperity, and success—" magnificently *prepared* for the long littleness of life." The rapidity with which he established himself in the City, the ease with which at an earlier date he did everything he wanted to do on a small income, the readiness with which he passed from serious to jest and back again in con-

2

versation; even the dexterity with which in 1914 he mastered the duties and the rôle of a trooper, all testified to a nature abundantly equipped for the triumphs and trophies of a conventional career.

All this, as his friend remarked, forms a striking contrast with the other Algy, mystical, prophetic, turning away from the world joyfully and without regret. And here I should be inclined to suggest that the real interest and significance of his life are to be found. His was a deliberate choice, made with a full knowledge of all he was rejecting, the renunciation of one who had something to renounce, the cheerful self-surrender of a young man " who had great riches."

Algernon Hyde Villiers, the youngest son of the Hon. Sir Francis Villiers,[1] British Minister at Brussels, and of Lady Villiers, and grandson of the 4th Earl of Clarendon, was born on February 1st, 1886.

He held a scholarship at Wellington, and had always wished to be a soldier. But short sight intervened, and he proceeded at the early age of seventeen, with a History demyship, to Magdalen College, Oxford, where he graduated with double honours and became Librarian of the Union.

To his great disappointment, he failed to be elected to All Souls', and this decided him to renounce his intention of going to the Bar. In 1910, therefore, he entered the office of James Capel & Co., stockbrokers, and in the autumn of that year was given leave to accompany his friend Charles Buxton,[2] the first Head of Ruskin College, to America, on a delightful tour which included a hunting trip in Wyoming. It was soon after this that he experienced the one great sorrow of his life in the sudden death of this friend

[1] The Rt. Hon. Sir F. H. Villiers, G.C.B., G C.V.O., G.C.M.G., etc., now British Ambassador at the Court of Belgium.

[2] Eldest son of Viscount Buxton.

and companion, whose original character and high ideals profoundly influenced his mind.

In the same year he married Beatrix, only daughter of Mr. Herbert Paul, and in 1912 became a partner in the firm of Govett.

On leaving Oxford he had thrown himself enthusiastically into the work of his College Mission in the dreary region of Somerstown, which lies behind St. Pancras Station. Here he spent many evenings in company with several of his friends and contemporaries, helping to run the boys' clubs, "turning those rough boys into true men," as the Head of the Mission said. He had charge of what was called the "Coalies" singing-class in the autumn of 1913, and it is good to know that these coal-heavers were among the first to join Kitchener's Army.

To Villiers himself the declaration of war afforded a welcome opportunity for putting to the test his ideals of renunciation and self-sacrifice. It came as no surprise, and the breaking of the storm found him eager to take his share in the great ordeal. It had been a source of great disappointment to him, when he left Oxford, that he should have failed to become a member of the Inns of Court O.T.C., on account of that defective eyesight which no one would have guessed at but for his eyeglass, which, moreover, did not afterwards prevent his becoming a "first-class shot." August 1914 therefore found him untrained, and the path which lay so clearly before him beset with many obstacles. His firm, however, was most generous in immediately allowing him to offer his services, and after vainly trying to enlist in the Infantry, he succeeded in joining the Hertfordshire Yeomanry as a trooper, and with them went out to Egypt in the beginning of September.

"The grit and cheerfulness" he showed on that trying voyage in a crowded troopship won him great respect from his friends among the officers, and warm friendships among his fellow-troopers—great indeed was his delight, on a stormy day, at hearing himself called " a bloody good Samaritan."

There followed eight delightful months, during which he was promoted lance-corporal, and took part in the defeat of the Turkish attack upon the Suez Canal.

In February 1915, feeling that he had now gained the necessary experience, he accepted the offer of a commission in the Lothians and Border Horse, joining his new regiment in Scotland three months later.

The effects of malaria kept him at home for the next two years, during which his unfailing interest in and enjoyment of his profession mitigated his natural impatience at not being allowed to proceed overseas. He was promoted Captain early in 1917; but as by this time he had begun to despair of ever getting to the front as a Cavalry soldier, and his health was finally restored, he sacrificed his captaincy, transferred to the Machine Gun Corps, and went out to France in July, in command of a section.

Four months later, on November 23rd, while taking part in the glorious capture of Bourlon Wood by the 40th British Infantry Division, he was killed.

His body was laid to rest in the little cemetery of Anneux.

In the winter of 1916–17 Algernon Villiers had helped to run a Machine Gun School in East Lothian. " I have embarked on an interesting experiment lately," he wrote in January. " I got some of the leading spirits among the men together, and read them a paper I had written for the occasion on the value of the forces of the Unseen World in everyday life. Afterwards they talked quite freely, and it is proposed to repeat the venture, they bringing some of their friends, perhaps. I am writing a paper on Prayer to read to them. It was on the whole a great success the first meeting, and I had the sense of doing something extremely valuable to myself, and almost certainly useful to them."

Four papers were written, read, and discussed, and their publication now needs no apology. They lay no claim to literary excellence, being nothing more than a simple and lucid exposition of the author's religious views, especially framed to appeal to an audience of average, but not exceptional, intelligence. That they were successful in their appeal, and fulfilled the purpose for which they were written, is more than evident from the tributes paid to his " talks " (as he called them) by those who were so ready to listen to him. " I know we all felt the better of his teaching," wrote one of his men; " I counted him one of my best friends, as did all the other boys who were under him."

" We are all anxious to see you before you go," wrote another, just before he went out to France, " and we should like to have at least one more of those ' talks ' which we all found so uplifting at Prestonkirk. You may never know how much good you did then, but one at least of your old M.G.'s will never forget what you said."

His hearers had perhaps hitherto enjoyed few opportunities of turning their thoughts from the material to the spiritual side of life; they had little time or inclination for metaphysical speculation. They were none the less eager to profit by the religious experience of one whom they trusted implicitly as a leader, to whom they confidently looked for guidance in all matters connected with their profession, whose judgment and advice they had rightly learnt to value and rely upon.

If, as is clear, these lectures proved a source of

help and comfort to those for whom they were originally compiled, it may be assumed that there are many others, blindly groping for some gleam of light to dispel the darkness of these' latter days, who will be glad to share the privilege which that handful of machine-gunners found so precious. For such as these the present volume is published, in the hope that it may inspire and stimulate the thoughts of a circle of readers wider than that of which the moral and physical welfare was in his lifetime the author's special concern. When the Angel of Death is abroad, when his shadow darkens every home, and the beating of his wings is re-echoed in many a fearful heart, there is courage and consolation to be derived from the teaching of one who had sought and found that peace of God which passes all understanding, who had learned by experience, and by his own example proved, that to be spiritually minded is Life Eternal.

It is not my intention to paint a full-length portrait of Algernon Villiers, nor to attempt any meticulous analysis of his character. But I may be allowed to say something of him as a comrade and as a soldier, in both of which capacities I had good opportunities of judging him up to within a few days of his death. In times of peace we had spent many evenings together, when the keen discussion of every conceivable question, intellectual, literary, or psychical, gave scope for the unconscious display of his exceptional mental powers. He was of so affectionate a disposition, so full of gaiety, humour, and sympathetic interest, that one could not fail to fall a victim to the irresistible charm of his radiant personality. "No one could meet him even in law matters without a sense of goodness and happiness pervading the dull room," wrote one who had only seen him on business. And during the autumn of 1917 it was my good fortune to meet him in France, to walk and talk with him on occasions, alas! all too rare, the happy recollection of which is one that Time can never dim. There was surely no more delightful companion than he; he was so widely read, he had such an excellent memory, his conversation was always stimulating and suggestive, his interest in the social and political questions of the day never flagged. He loved all the sweet, the sane, and simple things of life: little children, animals— without any " museum knowledge " he had made a special study of wild birds—the natural beauties of earth and sea and sky. Whatever was vulgar and base and stupid his soul abhorred, but he did not shun contemplation of the sordid facts of existence, facing them with an invincible optimism that proved his faith in the ultimate prevalence of good. His was, indeed, that purity of heart which blesses its possessor with a vision of the Divine in everything. He could talk about religion without self-consciousness, or that assumed air of solemnity which is commonly reserved for such discussions; he had none of Dr. Arnold's " manner of awful reverence when speaking of the Scriptures," and would not have denied to God the sense of humour and the gift of laughter of which mortal men almost unanimously claim the monopoly.

" Happiness and courage—those were the two things about him that caught my attention from the first, and will remain with me always as the distinctive marks of his rare lovable spirit," as a friend of his afterwards wrote. " With all his instincts for the arts and pursuits of peace " (wrote another friend), "he went *cheerfully* to war " (the italics are mine), " and made himself master of his part in it. His combined strength and gentleness were very winning; there was something very knightly about him. He stood for the very highest kind of duty and self-sacrifice."

The secret of his success as a soldier—for what is success but the perfect accomplishment of a set task, however humble ?—lay in the fact that he really took a keen delight in his work, that he was untiring in his devotion to duty, that he never spared himself in his efforts to secure the efficiency and promote the comfort of his men. By his example he did much to raise and maintain at a high level the tone of his unit. He exercised a profound influence for good upon his brother-officers, who regarded him with affection, mixed with a kind of deference which the two stars upon his sleeve could not account for, and of which he was, I am sure, totally unaware. He was indeed greatly surprised at the respect with which he was treated, " especially," as he said in a letter home, " when I remember the fact that I have been feeling very modest in my reduced position, and among the indomitable infantry men."

Modern warfare has been very justly described, from the point of view of the man in the trenches, as consisting to a large extent of periods of intense boredom and discomfort, punctuated, at more or less painfully frequent intervals, by moments of extreme danger and anxiety. It is not therefore greatly to be wondered at if, with rare exceptions, the soldier of to-day should be tempted to regard his military duties as an irksome and monotonous task in the accomplishment of which he is only upheld by a high sense of patriotism, by the traditions of military discipline, by *esprit de corps*, and that consciousness of the justice of a noble cause which renders any self-sacrifice possible, any degree of filth and fatigue tolerable. The Happy Warrior is rare for whom, as for Algernon Villiers, soldiering supplies an adventure almost pleasurable, rich in experience and interest, fraught with enviable responsibilities, a perfect medium for the very highest form of self-expression.

Villiers was indeed what is generally called a born soldier. For him the tedium and monotony of

military training had no terrors; as far as he was
concerned, they did not exist. In the early days
of his soldiering he displayed a remarkable capacity
for learning the technique of his profession, and later
on, as an instructor, proved himself to possess a
genius for imparting to others the knowledge that
a genuine interest in his work had enabled him to
acquire so easily.

To any fastidious man, as he undoubtedly was,
even to a fault, the squalor of trench life must always
appear intolerably distasteful; yet he never seems
to have been adversely affected by surroundings that
damped the ardour of less fervent spirits but could
not quench the flame of his inextinguishable enthusiasm. He was gifted, to a very notable degree,
with that saving sense of humour which helps men
to face untoward circumstances with a smile. "Above
all things," a fellow-undergraduate had said of him
long before, "he taught me that to carry on and do
your work was *fun*, if you cared to make it so." Villiers
cared to make it so, and found food for laughter in
trying situations, where others could only discover
reasonable cause for complaint.

There was something extremely infectious about
his zeal, his wholehearted and eager absorption in
whatever work lay to his hand, and no one could be
in his company for long without unconsciously re-
flecting the glow of his enthusiasm. To discuss
with him a question, social, political, ethical, or religious—and none loved a friendly argument better
than he—was, as I have already suggested, a purely
delightful experience. His views were always uncon-
ventional, often very original, and to doubt their
sincerity was as impossible as to question his own
conviction of their truth. Though essentially critical,
he was broad-minded and tolerant enough to listen
patiently to a statement with which he cordially

disagreed, and this mental attitude of his, combined with the clarity of his vision, the felicity of his language, and the power he possessed of putting his case logically and succinctly, made him a redoubtable but most charming antagonist.

" I have never met any one," wrote a friend of his, " who was nearer to God and the Truth. He seemed to have brought the whole of his powerful brain to bear upon the Teachings of Christ and his interpretation of them, with the result that he was able to live here almost as Christ's friends of His own day must have lived, in a peace and happiness that very few have even a glimpse of in this world. It was evident that his whole thoughts were centred in the search for Truth, and I am sure that he had found it as far as is possible in this state. I regard him as a prophet, for want of a better word, meaning by that that he had the spirit of God, and had been endowed with a wonderful gift of expression, by which he was able to convey his convictions to others. He must have been able to enlighten many people already, and if he had been able to stay here, he would have lightened the darkness of many more. Though his spiritual life was so strong, yet the human ties and his love for you all were as strong, and bound up in the spiritual life. It is all the same thing, of course, human love and divine. I do rejoice to have seen in him that it is possible to be a Christian and a good soldier—not that I had any doubt about it, but he is the most striking example I have seen."

Reading through his letters, and recalling the last talks I had with him, I think I am justified in saying that latterly he drew a new inspiration from St. Paul, whose personality had revealed itself to him with extraordinary vividness. But the example of Christ had been ever before him from the time when, as a boy at school, he used to say that the words in the Baptismal Service: " Christ's faithful soldier and servant unto his life's end," sent a thrill through him whenever he heard them. Far from that example suggesting a meek and mild attitude, it acted on him like a trumpet-call, as with that sturdy Apostle who fought with beasts at Ephesus, who urged his readers to put on " the whole armour of light," and to be " more than conquerors through Christ."

As he himself once said to a friend, he could never have faced what was ahead of him with such perfect equanimity, had it not been for the wonderful strength that he derived from a spiritual source. " He was extraordinarily happy in this way, and wished every one to share his happiness," his friend added.

To Villiers the presence of Christ was a supreme, a sublime reality. He had that sense of Communion with the Divine Power which proved a very present help in trouble. That God walked with him in the garden he was very sure, as sure as he was that nothing could separate him from the love of Christ. Thus armed, and fortified with this assurance, it is not strange that he faced death with perfect serenity, on the morning of November 23rd, 1917, in the great attack on the Bourlon Wood.

" I went to his guns just after dawn," wrote his senior officer, " and found him sitting under a bank —asleep. I woke him, and we talked over the Orders which he had had some hours before. We both knew he had a dangerous task to perform. He had read his Orders, decided on his plans, and gone off peacefully to sleep. He was extraordinarily happy, and as keen as a boy. I thought at the time how ready he was for whatever might come."

HARRY GRAHAM.

FRANCE, 1918.

II

1914

LETTERS WRITTEN FROM EGYPT AND ON THE JOURNEY OUT

HERTS YEOMANRY CAMP, CULFORD,
September 4th, 1914.

HITHERTO this adventure prospers. I was with noisy but genial dogs in the train. Their speech was not always very intelligible, and some of their jests altogether too tricky for my poor wits to follow. What would you have answered in my place if you had been asked whether you were growing a moustache? The correct reply is, " Rather," or " Not 'alf." So easy when you know it.

We got to Bury about 7.30. We walked a mile, and then squashed into the transport wagon, and had a glorious drive in the moonlight. I found some very jolly neighbours, and enjoyed it hugely.

We were to sleep in an immense barn about eighty feet long, with great doors letting in the moonlight. All round straw was spread, and covered with tarpaulins. I found a kit-bag for my head. I took off my boots and puttees, and put on a sweater. I can't say I slept very much, but no doubt more than I thought. At 5.30 gettings-up began, and then Trooper V. helped to clean and feed some horses. . . .

Breakfast of bread and jam and bacon, and then parade at eight. It is now 9.30. Between these

13

times I have led a sick horse before the officers, and led him back to his fence, tying him up nicely, and now I am sitting under a tree. . . .

When my hand is in, I know I shall enjoy this quite vastly. As it is, I am living with delicious keenness.

Saturday, September 5th.

Nothing very exciting has happened since yesterday morning. We spent the whole afternoon standing in the field here having our kit inspected and made up. . . . I slept much better last night, and the barn was really wonderful about ten o'clock when the men were all coming in and singing. It was splendid. I like my companions more and more. . . .

Sunday. STILL CULFORD.

We were all packed, and kit-bags were on wagons, at eight o'clock this morning, when we were told we should not go till early on Tuesday.

I am writing at sunset on a bridge in Culford Park. Behind me is the eighteenth-century stucco house, in front a lake from which a horde of ducks have just risen, and all around is their quacking, and the chirps of goldfinch gathering for Egypt, and all the loveliness of evening is matching my peace of mind. I have spent a little time in the church.

September 7th.

As soon as the day's work was over yesterday, I went off to Bury St. Edmunds, and had a good hot bath and dinner. That was why I did not write. It was the wildest luxury to sit on a chair. The food here is pretty loathesome. The tea is undrinkable, and I can only struggle with one lump of the daily stew, but I live on bread-and-jam, and buy chocolate and milk from the farm. The light of day is going,

14

and the one candle which lights us to bed, about sixty of us, would be useless for this, so goodbye. I am enjoying all the horse-coping more and more.

September 8th.

To-day recruits did musketry drill. It is by no means "so blooming easy," but after another time or two we shall be all right. At the moment the rifle —which is only a fraction bigger than the weapon I had in Wyoming—seems full of notches which catch on one's clothes whenever possible.

The horriblest job I have yet had is being (with another) troop orderly. This means fetching the cooking-pots . . . and when finished with they have to be cleaned for the next meal. That is horrible. The cans are called "dixies," presumably from their unutterable blackness, which is only equalled by the greasiness within. One's hands get into a ghastly condition. . . .

It is awfully hard to keep one's clothes at all clean with dixies and stables and oily guns, and a diet of bread-and-jam, consumed in close conflict with the wasps, which are legion.

s.s. "IONIA." *September 10th.*

I have been strictly truthful in all I have said so far, nor will I now conceal the fact that this may be Hell. Our quarters are very nice and clean at present, but they are the converted hold of a big cargo and passenger steamer, and should it be rough, and the portholes have to be closed, the air must become terribly bad. We shall sleep in hammocks above the tables where we feed. That will be a strange experience in itself. I must tell you the air-cushion is A1, and I have been sleeping like a top. Don't talk about a commission till I am an efficient trooper. You are right, I am very happy.

ALGERNON HYDE VILLIERS

So far this has been an amazing, though rather a terrible experience. Let me say at once that thanks to Mothersill, or I would rather say to God's grace helping me if the Kaiser had not desecrated the language of faith, I am triumphantly well in rough weather and mightily close quarters. '. . . I must say the appearance of our quarters was terrifying. On the lower troop deck, where I am, the central shaft conveys a certain amount of light. The portholes are about 10 feet apart, and 9 inches across. The whole place must be about 10 feet high, and narrow tables with benches project from the walls on every side. These tables are the locations of the various messes—twenty men each. Here we eat, and have severe blood to the head in so doing, and here at night the hammocks are slung. Some people slept on deck last night, but even so we were packed like sardines. Besides ourselves there is a whole regiment of Lancashire Terriers on board, and some gunners and R.A.M.C. We are said to be 3,600 in all, which is a lot too many. The first night I was called out to go on guard, and then told I wasn't wanted. I was too late to get a hammock, so I placed a blanket on the mess table, and with the air-cushion on my haversack for a pillow, I slept splendidly for eight hours, with an electric lamp exactly two inches from my head. Wasn't that a triumph? A glorious dawn showed four noble warships convoying us down the Channel. There was a rendezvous at the Eddystone lighthouse, where we hung about all the afternoon, and finally mustered fifteen strong under convoy of a battleship, the *Ocean*, I should think a pretty old one, and another small ship-of-war. Unluckily one of the fifteen is a wretched tramp which is carrying ammunition and can only go nine knots, so we have to go slow too, and Heaven knows when we shall make an end of it.

This morning the day broke pretty dirty, a good deal of sea running, and perpetual bursts of rain making the poor flocks of khaki sufferers very wretched. I took Mothersill at once, stood on parade like an old soldier, and not only enjoyed a good dinner of plain soup, potatoes, and some bread-and-jam, but was able to volunteer to get the food from the cook's galley and help in the washing-up. Luckily the lot did not fall on me to do this permanently through the voyage, and to-day there were not many to wash up for. The condition of the ship this morning on deck and below was beyond anything. . . .

On parade man after man made for the side, and I hear it was fun for A squadron parading on a lower deck aft of us. There is some grousing, but the real sufferers are mute. I have tried to help some of them, but there is really nothing to be done except when one can fetch them some bread, and so spare them a descent to the inferno. The decks present an extraordinary sight. Nearly every one is lying down in the rain, or with what shelter they can get from a deck cabin or a boat. The officers have allowed us to invade a portion of their promenade deck.

Some lie clasped together, and many holding hands, and their poor green faces might be those of dead men. If it were really rough, and we were all kept below, then indeed it would be Hell. The food is much better, and the service cleaner, than at Culford. In all these long and painful hours, with horrors which if not the worst are real enough all around, and threatening to engulf oneself in misery, I am able to feel happy in profound thankfulness, and to rejoice in the sense that in this and whatever may follow there is real desperate need of God's help and protection, and that if one gets through all right, then indeed there must be Someone looking after one. " He that keepeth thee will not sleep."

ALGERNON HYDE VILLIERS

September 13th.

The Lord's Day. Writing these words will probably be my sole recognition of this Sunday. If we forget, His property is always to have mercy, and so it is to-day, for the sea seems to be going down, and the sun has just come out. The sufferers are much more cheerful. They had a bad time last night. Tea-time is about 5, and when I had had mine I took a loaf of bread on deck to see if any one wanted food. You should have seen how they came for it. I made three trips back to the messes, and in all I must have cut up and distributed a dozen loaves. The men who two days ago were swearing and bucking and bursting with life now lay in prostrate droves before me, and feebly raised a hand or a faint cry for a crusty bit.

This evening the sea has really got quite calm. A good many people still wanted their tea brought to them, and lots of people were doing it. I have read a good deal of Boswell to-day. My funny little Corporal A. was thrilled by finding what book I had. He is a great admirer of the Tour in the Hebrides. He is a good fellow, an example of the nice, serious, half-educated dwellers in semi-detached houses on the Great Eastern Railway. He gave up reading fiction at twenty-one. I could not help saying I thought that was an error, as he was without knowledge of my two favourites, Jane A. and Borrow. However, he had me with his knowledge of Bacon's Novum Organum. I don't think he really can have understood much of it. Another fellow of somewhat similar type called B. is a scout-master, and also lives in Essex. Both wear pince-nez. B. is more voluble and priggish than A. Scouting is an eggy business, I fear. Thank goodness, neither of them are in my section; they would soon drive me to a frenzy, which I should bitterly regret. I like rather more

18

ruffianly fellows, I am sure. There is one type which is worse than the "wretched meritorious B.'s," and that is the schoolgirl type. There is a fellow called C. who is what one would have called an out-and-out squealer at Wellington. When he is one off you at parade he touches you on the shoulder round the intervening man, and pretends it was not he when you look round! Altogether intolerable! And had he not been taken ill last night, I should have been obliged to speak to him seriously, and possibly to punch his head for him. P.S.—I have had no more of this.

Monday, 14th.

It is quite lovely to-day, and the flotilla slowly steaming to the southward over a barely moving floor of deepest blue is a beautiful sight. . . .

Tuesday, 15th.

It is deliciously calm, warm, and sunny to-day. Our good fortune is wonderful. We hope to be at Gib to-morrow. Last night I slept on deck. It was not so comfy as in the slung hammock, but it is infinitely fresher and jollier than in the infernal hold. It was wonderful this morning to open my waking eyes on the red sun just peeping out between the horizon and a low bank of clouds. For an unexpectedly short moment he was the jewel on a glowing band of colour, and then slipped up and was gone.

The evenings, too, are beautiful when the two lines of transports east of ours are all glowing in the darkened sea. Later the stars come out and the ships of this fine flotilla begin to show their coloured points of light, putting on their diamonds and rubies for the night figures of the endless quadrille. Now the sea has gone down the dance goes at a better pace.

I have made my first real floater. We were *paid*

this afternoon (9*s.* on account) and dismissed. I then proceeded to shave, and have a thorough wash. As I was alone in the wash-house I heard a bugle call and a bell ring. I thought it sounded as if the ship were on fire, but really paid little attention. Bugles don't play any part with us. I remember thinking I should soon hear more about it. When I went down to tea, great questioning was made about my absence from parade! It seems it was a practice false alarm because of the German cruisers rumours.

I have twice seen birds not gulls, which for lack of glasses I could not make out. I should say shear-waters if pressed.

September 16th.

We are steaming in perfect weather over the most famous waters of history. We are showing a proper sense of the great names St. Vincent and Trafalgar, though I did hear a senior officer of I know not which squadron telling his men that Nelson was in command on the former of those immortal days. Major ——, wisely confined his remarks to Trafalgar, and was only a hundred years wrong in the date.

Last night and this morning I had a most damnable job to do. I was told off to a fatigue party whose business it is to get provisions up from the hold, and convey them to the proper parts of the ship for use. This morning we worked from 6 to 9 without having had a bite since 5 p.m. the evening before. We missed breakfast, but luckily got a loaf and helped it out with a little chocolate which I had in store. It was hard work too, pulling on a great rope which was like holding fire in one's hand, and well showed the futility of "thinking on the frosty Caucasus" in such circumstances. The deck was swimming in slush, and the rope made one in the foulest mess. The "stuff to be shifted" was mostly beer and ginger-beer for the canteen, and as I never look at either I had no enthusiasm for the job. I also carted bleeding crates labelled " ox-liver " into the most frightful recesses of the midships, where I suppose it will become our dinner. Not mine under the circs., I'm after thinking. I don't want that job again, but I am glad to say I was well able to bear my part, and took pleasure in working hard at it. A foul-mouthed old sergeant presided, and distinguished me by most courteous observations on the supposed unfamiliarity of such tasks. Broadly speaking, I find I am treated rather differently from the others. . . . A good many fellows call me Mr. Villiers or Sir, which I very much discourage. . . . I tell you all this as it is interesting from a general point of view, but also, I think, on the whole, though it is no doubt all wrong, I am grateful that it should be so. Things are made easier for one, and it would be affectation not to be glad of that. Kindly fellows and good comrades, I like being with them. . . . Yet of course I am utterly alone in many ways. When those birds come, and no one cares, I feel it. . . . Often too in the crowded nights and hours of leisure, when I have nowhere to go and write to you away from the unending stream of senseless jabber, then indeed one feels lonely in the presence of so much inevitable company.

I have felt lately, more than ever before, conscious of God's help, and the safety of my all in His hands. It seems as if I had given Him my soul, and He had given me His peace, which is indeed beyond understanding. Must not we therefore say that we should seek God where He can be found, and not rest content to live in separation from His Love and Power ?

GIBRALTAR, *September 17th.*

I must at once begin another letter to you now that my first has got safely started on its long journey.

I have been very seedy to-day as a result of
the inoculation. . . . However, I am feeling more
like myself this evening, and better able to enjoy
this wonderful blue bay, drenched in light, crowded
with the ships of our flotilla, and dominated by the
Rock. . . . The colours of these southerly places
are, as you know, rather monotonous at this time of
year, and the buildings all plain rows of windows in
the prevailing sandy tint; but now the sun is going
down, one gets more variety, and the masses of dark
green on the Rock's face begin to tell. The harbour
is full of little boats rushing about amongst us. I got
some grapes at dinner-time, which were delicious.

The worst of the overcrowded state of the ship
just now is that the canteens are almost inaccessible,
and generally sold out when at last one gets near the
window. There seems to be no more chocolate, and
jam is hard to get. The middle-day meal of soup,
meat, and potatoes is good, and so would the others
be if we could only buy something to help the bread
down. . . .

September 18th.

I have been feeling gradually better all day, and
now about 4.30 I am quite getting back my *joie de
vivre.* You will be glad to hear that the canteen ran
short of beer this morning, so that I and my mess-
mates all laid in a store of jam. I do think the dry
and wet canteens ought to be distinct, so that virtuous
jam eaters should not be kept from their harmless
little luxury by the hundreds of beer-bibbers. How
they can drink it on board and doing nothing I can't
think, but I suppose it is a deep-rooted habit with
most of them.

Saturday, September 19th.

This day is notable as my first " on guard." . . .
I got a rotten post down on the lower deck troop by

the cells. It was awfully hot but interesting. There was a prisoner in one of the cells. What he had done I am not sure. There were two versions. One was that he had lowered himself by a rope for a swim in the sea. Another was that he had been caught gambling below, been told to report himself every half-hour, and failed to do so. He was one of the Lancashire men. The cells are made like a loose box with the upper iron bars going to the ceiling. I could see the prisoner lying in a wooden bunk. He was a neat little man, with prettily-shaped hands and a gold ring on one of them. At 10.30 a sergeant came down with two others and marched him off. I believe he was going to be tried. During my two hours he did not come back. My duties were to keep people away from the cells, see that a drinking-tap was properly used, and that no smoking or gambling went on. I felt the tremendous authority of military law behind me as I said, "Keep clear of the cells there," and in a little dialogue like this with a party of mess orderlies who started playing cards. "No playing for money here, you boys." "A' right, only playing for love." "Don't let me hear the chink of money, then." "A' right, a' right." No doubt they were gambling, but not a sign of it could I detect.

About 11 the headquarters staff came to us on their rounds. A trumpet sounded and down came the regimental sergeant-major. Then followed the ship's captain—a pot-bellied old Tom in ducks with a thin nose like a parrot's beak in profile—our colonel walking rather gouty, and a string of a dozen officers and N.C.O.s. You should have seen how they sweated. The old buffers were mopping for all they were worth. Two complaints were lodged, about the tea and about insufficiency of rations. A long discussion ensued, and a Tom in white ducks was fetched and questioned. One of our officers came up to me and asked me about the tea, of which he said every one was complaining. I said I was no judge, as I never had sugar and therefore never had any of the tea. He was rather a nice fellow, I thought. Finally they decamped, to my great relief, as standing smartly to attention is heating, and in that airless region I was fairly trickling from every pore, and of course could not mop. The rest of my time was uneventful. I sweated less towards the end.

Our midday meal was brought to us here, and I have since been talking very happily with two extremely nice men. One is a traveller in nautical instruments and has been in many countries. He lives near Gorhambury. The other is a farmer near Broxbourne. We mentioned politics, and I found them both Free Traders.

The instrument man is quite intelligent. He has two daughters, about five and two, and is a great poetaster in his own estimation. Byron and Goldsmith are his favourites. The farmer is a delightful being, and told me a lot about his farm. He has 300 acres, and his principal interest is his herd of cows. I gathered he made a pretty good thing of it and has a dozen men under him. He has an old father whom he has left in charge. He has a charming graceful way with him which much adorns this ship's company.

We go on guard again from 4 to 6, from 10 to midnight, and from 4 to 6 to-morrow morning. Between times we must be here, where it is nice and cool. . . . I hope I shall get a better billet next time.

Sunday, September 20th.

I did get a much better post for my second bout of guard on the extreme stern of the ship. I had to keep men off a little area near the flag, and to keep a gangway free to the nearest companion ladder. When I first went on, the sun directly behind me was tremendous. It was not just hot on the back of one's neck, but like hot needles pricking one. By 5 the fierce quality was gone and the evening closed in the most serene peace of sky and water. Just before six o'clock behold two signallers and the colonel and adjutant came bustling up, and began frantic efforts to talk to the ship just behind us. I found out afterwards from a signaller that it was all about helmets, but from the fussification I quite thought German warships were about.

I had some food and sleep before 10, when I took up my post on the main open deck, again aft. About 20 yards farther down the deck was a row of huge cauldrons standing outside the main cook's galley, and pouring forth clouds of steam. The exhaust was evidently being driven through them. The clouds of steam had a fantastic air in the uneven light given by a few electric burners. Now and again they would suck to seaward, and I could see a fat man in shirt-sleeves sitting on a crate and holding a pack of cards. I suppose he was not playing "patience," but I could never detect his opponent.

After more sleep, rather disturbed by the lack of space and by rats and by the relief, which came off at 2, walking on one's face, we went on again at 4. This time I was guarding the forward galley, where a jolly Italian rascal, who smilingly presides over it, very soon started a roaring trade in hot tea and coffee and sandwiches at 3d. a head. It must have been quite illicit, as the goods can hardly have been his to sell, but I was mightily glad of some coffee, as a wind had got up and it was chilly. As the light began to come the hose threatened the forward deck, which I cleared of sleepers. The men sleep very peacefully and silently on deck, many of them in Charles's darling attitude of head and arm, but with all the difference!

Before my watch was out I had some very interesting talk with an old soldier who had served in India and South Africa, and joined the ———— with some friends of his recent civil life. He told me that his officers and N.C.O.s were perfectly futile. The colonel is secretary to the Board of Guardians in ————, and is hopeless. There are four sergeant-majors who are old regulars, but they cannot officer a battalion. The old Terriers know very little more than the recruits, and have got into bad disciplinary ways in their picnic camps, which make them very much worse material. . . . K.'s army would be very much better stuff to work on in all probability.

It is nearly 3, and a cool breeze is flicking the water with white crests as it tumbles joyously about, abounding in its own marvellous blue. When one thinks of the grizzly cruel masses of the Atlantic, this is like a laughing lake.

Church this morning was agonisingly funny as only these things can be. The band was in the waist and we on the promenade deck, and the version of " Fight the good fight " became a contrapuntal duel between us and the Lancs. They having the band were bound to win; " Victrix causa deis placuit sed victa Catoni," and we enjoyed our independent version as long as we could hold it more than they can have relished a tame obedience to the drum-major.

One is so helpless when bottom dog, unable to command things in one's ordinary, I now see to be, glorious fashion, and also particularly in one's complete ignorance. There is no means of knowing where we are, what we are going to do, *e.g.* stay at Malta or not, or why things happen. Endless idle rumours run around, and one realises that one is only a bit of a machine and not meant to be too inquisitive. These little drawbacks don't mean much, however.

It was delightful to find to-day that old Z. in my section has a profound reverence for E. G.,[1] and was thrilled to hear I knew him.

Who do you think has been on board these last two days ? None other than Turtur-turtur-turtur,[2] and I have seen a little bird which might be a gold-finch !

Tuesday, September 22nd.

Yesterday was very uneventful, calm and cool, and ended near Malta. I did not write, because I had not realised, through being on guard all Saturday, that the now regular 5 p.m. parade carries one into the dark hours. The principal event of the day was the discovery that a winked-at hot bath in the officers' quarters is to be enjoyed for *6d.* to the steward. The bath was too delicious. The luxury of reposing in the actual bath is very great, for though I no longer realise the hardness of the benches below or the deck above, they do not give one a positive sense of comfort! Then to get thoroughly clean from about a fortnight's dirt was wonderfully refreshing. . . .

I hardly eat any of the meat foods. Yesterday, *e.g.*, we were given liver sausages—quite disgusting and surely very unsuitable. To-day a sort of hunk of mule which was quite cold. It is, I imagine, better so, for soup and bread can't put one far wrong, and as we take very little exercise, one is in no great need of heavy meals. I enjoy the quarter of an hour's exercises every morning thoroughly. . . . Later this morning we did some semaphore, at which I rather distinguished myself. I have pretty well mastered it for the moment, at any rate. . . .

The voyage is beginning to hang heavy on one's hands, and Alexandria will be very welcome. In the

---

[1] Viscount Grey of Falloden.
[2] Turtle-dove.

meanwhile Boswell is a great prop. The farther on I go the more I like it, and I am going very leisurely, savouring the amusing things on every page. This sentence struck me as just hitting off my present case: "Men will submit to any rule by which they may be exempted from the tyranny of caprice and chance." These are truly the brokers' tyrants. Last night I talked with a young man who is heavily depressed by the discomforts of his position at this moment. I found out what life he had left. He told me he was a farmer and that his principal business was buying horses in Ireland, breaking, hunting, and selling them. I was better able to understand his disconsolate mood. . . .

Four o'clock. A wonderful sight—the Indian Army for Europe is just passing us to the south'ard —twenty-two great liners and a cruiser with them. Added to our own numbers it is a great display of sea-power, and all this is made possible by gallant, patient Jellicoe in the North Sea. The thought of the Sikhs and Gurkhas knifing *les sales Alleboches* gives me intense pleasure. They'll fight like devils, I dare say, and let the enemy know what it means when you take on the British Empire. Almost daily in these times one feels the great resources we are slowly displaying to drive home victory to the utmost. One must hope for this, mustn't one, though it sounds vindictive, and in the end I believe our English system of life, on which conscription is so hard to graft, may turn out to be the best and the determining factor in this deadly business.

Thursday, 24th

To-day we paraded half an hour earlier and stood to attention with our caps off, while the engines were stopped, to honour the burial at sea of a man of another battalion of Lancashire Fusiliers, who died on the *Aragon*. This is the third death which has occurred on the voyage, and, because of our having men of the same regiment as the dead on board, the most noticeable to us. In the other cases, one observed the stopping of the ship for a few moments, the flags half-mast, and the superstitious turn from their course of the ships following that from which the burial took place, that they might not go over the spot where the body was committed to the water. Among so large a number of men in unfamiliar circumstances, such casualties are sure to occur. The only case of which we know the particulars is that of a man who fell down a hatchway into the hold and broke his neck. It is a pathetic ending to the military vows of these three, to die on board and rest under this lovely azure floor. . . . Pray for me that I do not lose the sense of needing God's protection at every turn, and the happiness of leaning on His strength. Pray too, that I may maintain the principle of unselfishness, and help to set an example of kindness and of thinking about others before myself, if possible. This is a great source of happiness, and sorely needed to be done in a society where there is a tendency to admire the man who looks out for himself. One is told that this is what one must do, and it is quite true that every one must fend for himself and see to his own needs. But this emphasis tends to make men indifferent to the fate of others and has, I think, helped to produce a most noxious epidemic of petty thefts.

I was a victim to-day. I found my puttees gone from their usual nook. Fortunately for me, there are two who would help me, if need be, by lending me a pair. But losing one's kit in any way is an offence, and the stealer simply wished to push that offence of his making off on to some innocent person.

I have been lucky in making friends with all sorts

on the voyage, and feel sure they will stand me in good stead in all kinds of ways. At the same time, I have made no particular pal or chum, and don't really feel the need of one.

Later.—My puttees have been returned. They were taken by a genuine mistake, I'm sure. This has greatly cheered me. I am looking forward to the disembarkation.

Sunday Evening. ABBASSIA BARRACKS.

We got into Alexandria first thing on Friday and were berthed opposite a long row of coal mountains. The whole ground was made of coal dust, and about midday the heat and filth were awful. I was put on " a fatigue " (of which life largely consists) to unload our stuff and put it on the train. We had no helmets. Mercifully, after an hour our second-in-command came and put some natives on to the job. They put us into the train drawn up between us and the coal at 5 o'clock. We were allowed to get out and stay near by. After a time we four—the section—started out in search of a rumoured pub. Very soon X. and Y. got funk and said we were going too far, but old Z. and I stuck it out and had rather a lark wandering among weird quays in the half-dark, though we never found the pub. The officers were obviously having dinner. We two raided the deserted ship, now bound for India to fetch home more men, and did very well to get drinks of milk and a big pot of jam in sub-terranean regions. Food and drink are one's supreme objects. It is very primitive and amusing. There was a cataract of hot water coming from the liner and running over the quay and down a hole. Here we all washed in the far-away light coming from the ship, and not intended for us. At last at 9.30 the train went off. It was quite impossible to sleep, and we were very much jammed with all our accoutre-

ments and kit, but we ate much bread-and-jam to
keep us going. At one station there was lager beer
and a regular rush for it. It fetched 1*s.* a bottle,
and by gum it was good. I stood out on the tail
platform a good deal. It was a lovely night and the
starlight exquisite. Then one looked inside. What
a contrast! The dreary burners in the thick air
showed the men and their stuff in every attitude of
hideous discomfort. Some on the floor—others sang
and smoked.

We got out here to the Abbassia Barracks at about
4.30 just as the dawn was coming, and marched off
in the growing daylight to our quarters—beautiful
airy dormitories with verandas north and south, just
as good as could be, with shower-baths and glorious
Dragoon Guards welcoming us to breakfast.

September 29th.

We are beginning to settle down a bit now, and I
mean to take up again my plan of writing every day
a running letter; . . . the fact that one has not got
to finish off and make a letter of it each day rather
adds to the pleasure of this mode of intercourse.
Now where shall I begin? Our arrival here is the
point, I think. In the first rays of daylight, as we
got out of the train, the feature was a mosque-like
building which I remember bothered my eye by
being distinctly out of drawing in the minaret part.
This is the central feature of the newer and eastern
part of this regular settlement of barracks. . . . In this
region all the barrack buildings are alike, exactly
the colour of the sand and three big stories high.
The colonnades on each side of each floor are really
quite fine, and delightful in use. . . . To the south
and east we have a sight of the fringes of the desert.
It is thrilling to see even the edge of this great thing
in nature. It is just a colour to the east. Very low

ridges come first, and then a purple or violet vanishing into the sky. In the south the stony hills rise quite quickly and glow a bright red at times. Some people have found the light very trying—others the sand, which is all-penetrating. I don't really mind the heat a bit, and the light and the air are too wonderful for anything. The sunshine is a blaze or a flood, or anything else which can suggest a gorgeous profusion. The air is lightness itself, into which shapes and colours cut with a clearness and vigour which give a beauty to the simplest bush or building. It would be terribly hard to make a sketch of anything. The sky at night is a wonder. As I look up through the columns, the stars are like a diamond network over the world-wide curtain of sumptuous blue. Sometimes it looks black like a superb creature's coat—a Bagheera black. For a moment at sunset the light which has been poured out all day rushes back from the earth to the sky, and both glow in a level glory. Descriptions are no use. It is just a glorious climate.

October 1st.

. . . As to grooming, I enjoy it hugely, and do not find it hard at all. You can work just as hard as you like at it, and I enjoy putting in the elbow-grease. It is so satisfactory to see the result in a glossy coat, fresh face and feet, and air of well-being in the brave beast. Besides my own already beloved animal here, I have groomed about four or five others, and always with skill or luck as to quietness. Being repeatedly in the stable every day gives one great assurance. I should like to live to be a hundred for hunting and stalking.

Friday, October 2nd.

I rode my horse this morning with complete success. He is a darling, and I am as pleased as Punch about it all. . . .

The soldier's spirit as one sees it here, and as I read of it yesterday in *Lloyd's Weekly*, is a remarkable compound. Things that really matter are taken with calm, while the grousing and cursing over trifles is unending. For instance, sea-sickness and that night journey, and the following night's trek to Cairo were all taken exceedingly well; but you've no idea of the outcry there is if anything goes wrong with the rations, or the canteen runs out of jam or beer. If we heard we were to go into action this evening, there would be hardly any agitation; but suppose it got about that 1*d.* a day was to be stopped from our pay to (say) keep our kits in repair free of charge, or some such convenient scheme, the to-do would be fierce and interminable. The tea and the cooking of the meat arouse the most bitter passions. You would say superficially that we worshipped the Belly with whole-hearted monotheistic devotion.

This moment I have just had my first sight of the Pyramids! It is marvellously clear to-day, " sharp as a sickle is the edge of shade and shine," and C., standing at the end of the veranda suddenly, said, " There are the Pyramids." Planting this safely under a mustard-pot, I rushed off, and there they were— fourteen miles away to the west the two immortal masses, wonders of the world.

Later.

After tea I started for a delicious walk from which I am just back. . . . The moon was well up in the sky when I went off, but the gorgeous sunset light was still the master. I went over to the lines of the camel corps. The ships of the desert lay in four long lines of about twenty-five or thirty each, chewing with their peculiar air of indifference, very unlike our restless steeds. The camel corps have evidently got one of the early parts of the barracks and the scene was fully Pentateuchian. There was the round well-head with the two short thick foliages trees beside it, and as I came by an Arab began his prayers. The camels who came in to-day from work in the desert lay very solemn and still, white-brown and dusty coloured, waving their heads, and now and again one would get up with much deliberation, turn round, and lie down again. Beyond them I came to some old fortifications with big guns of Napoleon's time in their old positions. Farther on there was a pleasant-looking residency of some sort with a grove of poplar trees, and beyond the open desert. I looked out over it for a time stretching away under the brilliant moon, and two men riding arabs went by inaudibly perhaps 200 yards away. I came home through other Egyptian Army quarters to find a glorious donkey-race going on near the barracks.

ABBASSIA. *October 12th*, 1914.

Yesterday there was a good deal of light left when we got back to barracks. So A. and I set off to walk out over the desert to the " south'ard." The desert is full of incident. Old trenches, dried-up streams where the sand is caked hard, odd little bushes, outcrops of rock, and glowing to our right a gorgeous sky burning from yellow to orange and orange to smoky red behind all sorts of dim architectural features, chief among them the dome and pinnacles of Arabi Pasha's citadel. We crossed a crazy-looking railway-line which vanished up a sandy valley in front of us and found a curious enclosure—an old fort or caravanserai at the foot of the hills. We climbed the lowest slopes of these, and wished we had had more light for the northward view. But still it was very beautiful and utterly unfamiliar. I don't seem to have got any grip on the landscape. It is still quite *en dehors*. It was dark in a few minutes, and we came home by the guide of the barrack lights which shone in steady regiments in front of us. It was a good walk.

I have had extremely nice letters from Sybil Graham[1] and hope to go to luncheon with them on Wednesday. She is lending me some books, as I want a change from Johnson! He doesn't suit barracks as he did the ship. On Sunday morning after breakfast I read through Ecclesiastes and the Epistle to the Ephesians. It was splendid to come from the pale exquisite beauty of the weary philosopher to the triumphing apostle. And how beautiful he can be too: Be ye kind one to another, tender-hearted, forgiving one another, even as God for Christ's sake hath forgiven you.

October 13th.

An unlucky day too. Last night in the course of a battle with No. 4 troop across the way I had a violent blow on the head from a stoutish bolster powerfully wielded, and I think this spoilt my night. . . . An interesting thing I have been meaning to mention is the great flights of hawks which fill the air above the barracks at meal times. They tell me the birds are Indian kites, not native here but imported from India as scavengers. They are not handsome, but their numbers and quaint whistling noise are very striking. I have noticed very little else in the way of birds.

Thursday, 15th.

Immediately after stables I made myself as presentable as possible and went off to luncheon with the Grahams. It was desperately good to be in a lovely cool dark house full of nice things, and to talk at large with one's own sort of people. They gave me a lot of papers and books and were altogether more

[1] The Hon. Lady Graham.

than kind. She drove me home in a motor by way of a colour-man's shop, where I got the materials for some sketching. No sooner was I back than I had to get ready for night stable guard. There was some straw to sleep on outside the stable guardroom, and we took down a blanket each. I was on from 9 to 11 and then from 3.30 to 6.

The prospect of controlling loose horses in our squadron's *three* stables frightened me, I must own, but all went well. One rascal, who was a sore trial to the man whom I relieved at 9, I managed to fix up all right and had no trouble. One soon gets used to going up to strange horses and seeing they are properly fixed. It was also rather eerie patrolling the dim stables all warm and lined with shadowy horse-forms in a half-silence of moving and munching, broken by sudden loud noises when one animal got up from a lie-down, and indulged in a kick or two at his neighbour. Outside the stars were blazing, and a young crescent moon sailed along, showing the buildings and trees and troughs in a new fantastic aspect.

October, 7th.

It is magical to read of the conduct of our troops. Why are they like that? M., in a very nice letter, speaks of my having no excitement of battle to compensate me for giving up my ordinary life, but adds that something much deeper than mere excitement must be animating our soldiers. I wonder what that is? We *understand* of course that we must beat the Germans, but one would suppose some deeper-seated motive power necessary. Do you meet with any passion? Among my comrades there is not a trace —nothing even faintly resembling Chabanne's[1] fine fury. Yet I think when and if our turn comes, the

---

[1] His brother's French chauffeur.

needful will be done, not without "grousing," but yet done perhaps as well as any men could do it. However that may be in our case, the stories from the front suggest that there is a power of faith working in our Army. The men have faith in their officers, the officers implicit faith in their religion of sportsmanship. "Play the game" is a phrase which may be eggy in peace times, but is absolute law now.

I take it some faith is the foundation of all great or good life. The search is ever for a more comprehensive form of faith, isn't it? which will always work and make all life great and good.

Tuesday, 20th.

On Sunday I spent a most pleasant afternoon and evening with R.

We went up to Mohammed Ali's citadel, covered by the mosque which he had built in the Italian style! The native output of builders was by then reduced to nothing and foreigners had to be got for work of this size. The effect of the Palladian mosque is pretty bad and some of the details are hideous. The lights were lit in hundreds, and produced as one went in a sense of flatness which was curious. All hung low above the red carpets spread over the vast unfurnished space—they illumine a great low expanse and leave the upper heights of the dome in semi-darkness. It was very unlike our great churches, where one always has the sense of height. Before going in we went out on to the terrace and watched a gorgeous sunset looking over the town, which lay in a dim semicircle at our feet. Beyond it lay the Nile, and beyond that the mighty Pyramids stood out even from here higher than the distant hills, so that their summits were cut against the fiery sky. It was a wonderful sight—a sea of domes and minarets all rising up to one,. and all in sight and sound so strange and so very old.

October 24th.

My faith is that what is coming to me is coming for a purpose. Trust God nor be afraid. Perhaps the purpose is for a new life, perhaps for a better grappling with the old, but we will wait for His guidance, won't we? One learns among the thousand lessons of this time to wait for orders and to accept them without question.

ABBASSIA. *October 25th.*

One of the many miseries of war is the confusion it brings. I remember French stories about '70 which made one feel the desolation brought by the destruction of the many little certainties on which we commonly depend. It is just when by the war we need them most that these things go, isn't it? and that suggests the only grain of comfort which one can get from this hideous state of things—that the true values of life emerge with irresistible clearness. There is a moral value in the great upheaval and the testing which all are going through, but I remember of old that I used to argue against Johnner that the destruction and ruin lasting on for generations, after the moral élan of a warlike effort was spent, more than outweighed the value of the latter. I am of the same opinion still. If one could really believe that a different world would come out of this struggle, one could be more hopeful. But I don't now see any good reason for the feeling one had in the first excitement that the old order was changing. Not by such means are the changes brought which matter. We shall go back to the same world with more antagonisms and a huge legacy of broken lives,, broken homes, and broken resources. Poverty will be greater and the hope of alleviating it dimmer. Still, there is for me at least a strong sense of the other side of the medal. . . .

I will try and set down after a month's trial what seem to be the really good things which this life is teaching me to recognise. I speak with full consciousness of the shortness of the trial, and therefore very " provisionally," and of the difficulty of making such things clear to oneself, still more to anybody else. First there is the delight of having quite definite new things to master. In every life one is always learning about new things. Here, however, they are gloriously defined—to ride and groom, to drill and shoot. Then there is the health of these simple things and the satisfaction of doing them. . . . One feels one's successes so keenly too—a horse under good control—a horse nicely groomed—a good bit of drill, and without doubt in time a straight shot—these are very *savoureux* things. The long and short of it all is, this is a man's life, and it does look as if by the sweat of his brow a man should live.

November 3rd.

The march through Cairo of the whole division was really a great success. The Herts Yeomanry and B Squadron, in particular, were picked out for applause by the General. We went right through the native quarter by narrow streets which we quite filled riding in sections, *i.e.* four abreast—past numbers of beautiful mosques under a heavenly blue sky. The native crowds were very large, and extremely clean-looking on the whole. They were very respectful and silent. There is vague talk of disturbance and martial law has been proclaimed in Cairo, but I don't think it amounts to anything. We have double guards at stables now and then, and carry bayonets which we don't know how to use, and no rifles to fix them to. Also, whenever I plot with the Robertsons to go to the Pyramids, we are confined to barracks, which is tiresome. . . . Staying here is no doubt rather a picnic, unheroic enough, but there it is, one can't do more than the powers decree, can one ? . . .

November 9th.

All your news of the war is most interesting. It does look as if the Germans had made a real bungle of the whole thing—right, left, and centre—and succeeded only in devastating Belgium, which every principle of decency and respect for what is of good report should have constrained them to spare.

" Their necks shall pay for all when they die." I am for the uttermost farthing of humiliation of the dynasty and people : consistent with not attempting to turn them by annexation into anything but their beastly selves.

MAADI   *November 28th.*

All day yesterday a horrible wind was blowing which smothered the whole sky and landscape under a film of mist or sand—a bit of both, I expect, and there was really nothing to be seen anywhere. This morning the hills were clear amethystine on the upper contours, fading into dreamy softness lower down, so that each ridge told sharply against the ridge behind it. The sun was heralded by a flying robe of glowing yellow folded with light clouds, and I sat entranced for half an hour trying to catch the loveliness of the dawn, till up came the sun himself and shone straight in my face. It was delicious, but I fear my sketch is not.

HÔTEL DES VOYAGEURS, ISMAILIA.
February 3rd.

I penetrated to the Flying Corps camp in search of Sam Cockerell, and we dine together to-morrow. He recommended me hither for a meal this evening. After the first quasi-normal meal since we parted, I feel vastly cheered up, and the fact of having a table and chair handy, not to mention such luxuries as pen and ink, clearly point to my seizing the opportunity of writing to you. If you could realise the extreme difficulty of life in a sand camp, especially at first— though, of course, I keep reminding myself that a sand camp must be heaven compared to a mud camp—I don't think you would expect much.

We have dug ourselves holes and stretched our waterproof sheets over the top to shelter us from the cold wind and very heavy dews. We have got a rather limited allowance of not very clean straw on the floor. Thus sleeping close together we manage to keep pretty warm. Isn't it bad luck getting this cold spell?

The food is conducted on the same principle as at Culford, only the meat of which the dirty stew is made is much better. There is a ramshackle canteen providing eggs, sardines, and oranges, and some German biscuits. The sand and the cold are our enemies, but one gets used to both.

Our long day was really thrilling. Of course from the soldiering point of view it was a great failure, as we saw nothing but a few dead camels and a little Turkish debris, but crossing the canal at dawn was glorious. It was the opening of a beautiful day. We went over a pontoon bridge and then joined the Indian cavalry. One could see their lances in front like a dim forest against the reddening east. Altogether I enjoyed it, though it was a little flat when an aero came and said the Turks were out of reach. Yes, it was a disappointment when the advance on the Friday night was given up.

ALGERNON HYDE VILLIERS

Our three days' glorious trek into the desert came to an end this morning. It has been a wonderful experience. . . . Soon after my last most unsatisfactory note I entrained for this spot. Jolly very kindly met me, or I should never have found my way across the Canal and through the trenches and wire entanglements to our lines. The Canal was thrilling.

The great ships following one another in the darkness with searchlights blazing at the bows. We crossed on a tiny ferry-boat. The point was guarded by Indian sentries, and one of their officers wanting to hurry the ferryman, called out to the guard on the far side using the true vocation " O Sentry," and then a sentence in Hindustani. I shall never forget that " O Sentry."

I got to sleep at 2 and we were up by 4. Our way led east, along a great caravan route where the sand of the desert has been hardened into quite a road by the feet of innumerable millions of camels. This is one of the highways " down into Egypt."

Along this road came Joseph, sold to the Ishmaelites, and then Jacob and his family, and by the same way Joseph and Mary made their flight.

At first the way was flat with a good deal of scrub, then the levels became more varied, and we passed little palm groves here and there. After leaving a bigger one, where we were to camp, we went on to quite a high ridge to protect the front while the infantry marched up and made themselves good for the night. We had with us the 14th Sikhs and some Gurkhas, the Patiala Lancers and part of the Bikanir Camel Corps. The Lancers, though a purely native regiment, have an English officer attached to them, a certain Captain Willis, who was really in command of the Cavalry.

Willis's headdress was exquisite—a turban with a

little grey-green pyramid sticking out, and the whole bound with a silk scarf of a moonlight green, the end of it hanging down over his shoulder. Beautiful being! his bewitching fragrant panache gave an atmosphere to all our dull, stiff-clad ranks when he sailed by on his long comfortable charger. All the Indians are beautiful. The Sikhs keep their clothing and arms so fresh and spick while the Gurkhas are the picture of nimbleness and dexterity. The Lancers did the advance patrols in a way which we mightily admired.

I was corporal of the main guard that night, protecting our precious ammunition and not less precious water. I enjoyed performing my duties, and I also had a better night than most—who had to go and sleep in trenches surrounding the lines. This appears to have been highly unpopular. We were up at 4.15 for Der Tag. The aero had reported small bodies at Katiah the day before, and we were to go and chase them out.

We watered in the palm grove at dawn—a picturesque but protracted business.

After a time X took out a patrol, and my section was detailed to maintain connection between him and Sergeant Jolly with the main part of No. 3 Troop.

X went fast, though the going was cruel heavy at first—reached Katiah—found no trace of a foe, rallied us and took us back to the main body by about 1.30. We then had a long march home to our palm-grove camp. No doubt the Turks have gone right away. There was not a sign of them.

The country all day was magnificent—great mountains of wind-smoothed sand with sharp, golden edges against the blue. The distances to the east were purple and greys at a range of mountains somewhere towards the frontier. Katiah is nothing but a flat, marshy stretch peopled by insects and a few herdsmen. Still, it's on the map! In all we did between thirty

43

and forty miles. I wouldn't have missed it for anything, though X thinks that probably there
vanished with it our last chance of using our rifles in
earnest.

This morning we came quietly in here, and go back
to Ismailia to-morrow bearded and dirty, but glad of
our luck, such as it was. The ponies have done excellently. Ismailia after this will be the limit.

III

LETTERS WRITTEN IN 1916 AND 1917

April 8th, 1916.

THE proposal finally to abandon the cosmopolitan idea in trade relations and embark on a boycott of Germany after the war is terribly foolishly wicked. As ——— so well said the other day, what we hope for and are fighting for is a new Germany, and to declare war beforehand on the unborn realisation of all our hopes is indeed to doom ourselves to a useless sacrifice.

From the earliest week of the war I have felt what a bitter irony it would be if our hideous combat with Prussia ended in our own surrender to Prussian ideas. It is the sort of thing that does happen. Cuckoos, like N———, are spell-bound by Germany as by a basilisk. Like old barndoor fowls, they cannot get their beaks away from the chalk line, and while we are in the very act of proving that the German way is fatally wrong, they will vow and swear that unless we follow the German way we must be lost for ever. To me it is beyond the bounds of rationality—like the ideas of lunatics. Forgive my ranting!

AMISFIELD. October 27th.

I have finished St. Paul's epistles and am putting down the leading thoughts of each, as I understand them, with the idea of finding out what it was that made the Thessalonians, etc., become Christians, and what St. Paul conceived Christ's revelation to be.

It is most fascinating work, and quite takes the place of sketching ! !

These last days have been lovely.

The skies have been softest greys, and moving gently towards the east.

The hills are looking very dark and solemn, and the hedgerows beautiful in their faded colours, like the Reynolds windows in New College chapel. . . .

I am going to Tynningham to see if there are any waders in.

November 17th.

Why did St. Paul become a Christian ? It was surely the power to live and die which he had seen in the early believers, and perhaps especially in Stephen, which led up to the paroxysm of revelation on the road to Damascus. In his own preaching that, I suspect, was the primary thing in approaching the unconverted —*e.g.* I Thess. i. 5, and I Cor. ii. 4. The Epistles have only allusions to primary teaching. They are in every case addressed to believers. Thus St. Paul seems to say, Here is a tremendous practical new fact—if you want the theory of it and the implications, here they are.

St. John writes as if he were by way of answering a more sophisticated questioning : How came this obscure life to be the initiation of so much—a church, a power to turn the world upside-down ?

The contrast seems to be largely one of date—St. Paul representing the full career of active Christian life ; St. John the later years, when a man turns back on his life, and recalls its beginnings into the full light of spiritual experience.

I try every day to realise this saying. Here the thing is proved beyond question of doubt—there *is* only one power, only one joy, only one health, only one goodness, only one pearl of great price, to seek honestly to be led by the Spirit of God.

It is a mathematical demonstration really (though oddly enough you can ignore it if you like—hence the pearliness), and none but an idiot would lose his own soul when once he has found it. The only reason we do not " believe in God " as completely as in $2 \times 2 = 4$ is that the subconscious self seems to carry on still in the old way, and can, so to speak, rush us and suddenly dominate consciousness quite unexpectedly—*Zu plötzlich.*

November 29th.

Horses would be no good to us now—bitter thought —there is hardly anybody left who could ride them. As I marched this afternoon, immediately behind my old gun men, my heart was wrung to think what fine fellows they are, and no finer than their former comrades. They are the last leaf of our summer pride.

I am, however, glad to say that it will fall with certitude and honour, for the Brigadier has warmly taken up my idea of their going to the mounted M.G.C. . . .

I was much interested to hear of your readings about the dark ages of the East. Life is indeed *hid* with Christ in God.

November 14th, 1916.

To N. B.

I think actually sharing one's thought with other minds keeps it saner and clearer and more vigorous than it would be otherwise.

Shall we agree not to use the word " matter " any more ? It is too full of rubbishy, outworn notions to be good for us. It needs a rest.

About animal decay your thoughts are excellent. Why should the poor microbes that change us one way be worse than those which change us the other ?

I am sure you are right in feeling that evil is in our thoughts. That's why we can get rid of it. And evil I take to be ignorance and limitation. Complete knowledge and complete power (si jeunesse savait, si vieillesse pouvait) would exclude or eliminate evil. I am entirely with you—all things are of God—the content of God's constitutive thought. To me it is equally misleading and confusing to call all things matter or spirit. So long as you grasp that the sun and stars, the tables and chairs, are both universal and particular, and have an existence, not dependent on our knowledge of them, but capable of being understood by us to be constituted by the All Mind, that is all you want to know about them from an existential point of view. As for the glorified replica and " the reflection " and " the true reality shining through," that is all perfect nonsense. There is one reality only, but it is not yet perfectly *mastered* (that's the word covering both intellectual and moral power—" Thanks be to God which giveth us the mastery ") by us.

Mrs. Eddy's English is indeed awful. I suppose that's where her followers get the idea of Truth shining through. She erects a pretty effective blanket, I must say.

Here then is *the* problem—" Why is reality not completely mastered by us ; why are we ignorant and limited ? "

I have got an attempt at an answer, which I will give you ; but some common notions must be dispelled first.

It is generally assumed that reality is indestructible, incorruptible. This means that reality is changeless and good. I think it is neither.

Reality more deeply considered is not merely God's

thought, it is God's *purpose*. In the idea of purpose you can account for the development, change, which we see so inevitably, and for the homogeneity without which we cannot be satisfied. In a divine purpose the End is immanent in every means. Perfection in every stage. "Each note of one scale is nought," " but give it to me to use." . . . " Consider and bow the head."

Then reality is beyond Good and Evil. Not only beyond evil, but also beyond good. It is Truth and Beauty probably, but not good. Good is a false absolute.

Look at Phil. iii. 7, 8, and 9, " I count *all* things but *loss* for the excellency of the knowledge of Christ."

All these wonderful passages, *e.g.* Col. iii. 11, " Where there is neither Greek nor Jew, circumcision nor uncircumcision, barbarian, Scythian, bond or free, but Christ is all and in all," what do they mean ? This, I take it—that not only what men hold evil, but what they hold good—race, creed, civilisation, status—all is done away in Christ.

Is not the life and teaching of Jesus the same ? " My meat is to do the will of My Father," and " Who are My mother and sister and brother ? " " They that do the will of My Father."

And the Cross—what of it ?

To me it is Truth and Beauty cutting good and evil to ribbons.

To return to *the* problem, then. Do you think this parable can stand ? The Kingdom of Heaven is like unto a great artist who made a picture of a man's head ; and he painted the shadows first, and the man said, What a puzzling picture, and ugly too ! But when the picture was finished, the shadows were still there. Yet the man hung the picture in his dining-room, and everybody said, What a likeness, and what a fine picture !

The shadows are our apparent ignorance and limitation, but when we have conquered them we shall know they are the embodying contrasts of our knowledge and power. Perhaps the old sillies who said that God sent us evil for our good were not *quite* so silly after all. It is a great mystery. I find in an old hymn —hoary theological—so much completeness and satisfaction:

> " O come in this sweet morning hour,
>   Feed me with food divine,
>   And fill with all Thy love and power
>   This worthless heart of mine."

I cling to my " sweet morning hour " and my " worthless heart."

There is truth expressed in both.

St. Paul does not mean that a natural body and a spiritual body exist together. The context makes this quite clear. Christ really died, but death had no dominion over Him, and the bird really decays and dies, and the leaves fall and flowers wither, but never mind, Death is *swallowed* up in Mastery.

December 7th, 1916.

I walked home by Hailes. It was really rather beautiful—not a puff of wind, and the horses creeping up the furrows the only signs of life or promise of renewal. Yet there they were in the still passing of the year, working for next year's golden October.

So, I thought, we must remember that deep in the core of life God's purpose works through the perplexities of German victories, and apparently inadequate statesmen, towards the harvest of souls.

The papers are hard to bear just now. There is only one thing to do—to turn away from the whole apparent failure of our efforts.

To E. P.

December 10th, 1916.

I think it is essential to remember that the distinction of outward and inward is very flimsy. Christ calls us not so much to a change as to a thorough *re-valuation* of life, inside and outside and all through.

I quite agree that " we are citizens of the world," and to seek to avoid common life in any way is as impossible as the Christian Scientists' effort to deny it—but as having the freedom of the Civitas Dei *we must not care* what may befall. Love is the supreme function of life, and it is natural that love should wish to see its objects happy, but love must not end there. We must welcome the whole will of God for ourselves and for one another—and what was the will of God for Christ, in Whose life alone His will was utterly fulfilled ?

It so happened after getting your letter that I read the account of Jesus' temptation. How was He going to use the tremendous power He now felt within Him ? Not to feed men, not to shelter men, not to govern men (which is what we so often think we should like above all things), for to change the existing order of life would be to imply that in the goods and evils of this life there is the possibility of reconciliation with God. Christ evidently decided to leave the facts of life as He found them and to show us by His life and death and resurrection how to understand and value them. His full insight showed that thus alone could He fulfil His mission. He quite clearly taught an indifference to human goods and a victory over human ills, and to my mind His example is in exact accord with such teaching. It is a familiar thought with me, but when I first met with it I do not know, that the striking thing about Christ's example is not His various " works," but the fact that with such power as He possessed He did so little and left the world practically as He found it.

Nothing, I think, is more sublime in Him than the absolute confidence He displayed in Truth and its power, which made Him quite indifferent how many He reached and healed. He needed only time enough to declare His message, His revelation of God's attitude to life, and to seal the truths of it by the complete experience which it involved. For the last week of His life, when if " works " had been His object He would have been seeking to do all He could to destroy " evil," He did no works of healing save Malchus' ear, so far as we know. Surely He would have plainly given men the key to health if that had been His mission. Rather He gave us the key to life, and in those last days was concerned to reveal by word and deed the deep things of God. " Render therefore unto Cæsar the things that are Cæsar's, and unto God the things that are God's." If people came to Him who had realised His powers, He could not but heal them. He does not seem to have sought them. Even in His preaching there is a complete absence of that urgency which is so characteristic of St. Paul. I am every time struck with this when I turn from the Epistles to the Gospels.

To E. P.

January 14th, 1917.

" Hope is Faith in action " is a telling phrase, but still Faith, whether in reflection of action, should remain Faith—the goal reached even in the pursuit ; whereas Hope is the beautiful expectancy, waiting for the fullness of revelation not reached even by Faith, which is clearly an element in the Christian character and which I can understand that St. Paul should rank with Faith and Love as the three which abide. This

is just where Beauty comes in. It is not a matter
of Faith, is it ? though we may well have Faith that
it is an ultimate thing. Beauty comes to complete,
with the seal or character of God in His fullness. We
wait for the hour when the King in His beauty shall
draw us in joyful surrender to be one with Him. The
foretaste comes to us in the pure passion for loveliness
" which leaves the earth to lose itself in the sky."

What you say about Christ and the æsthetic fact
in life is quite true. He does not teach the Beautiful
as He taught the Truth, because that is not the way to
convey it. He reveals the Beautiful by the faultless
grace of His earthly life and death. In a lyric of
bewildering beauty such as the twenty-first chapter of
St. John, is it not clear how some profound follower
of our Lord grasped the significance of the Resurrection
as the consummation, on this side too, of the Word
Who dwelt among us, and we beheld His glory full of
Grace and Truth ?

I wonder if you will think anything of the idea, but
it has been in my mind lately that we might be right
to associate our ideas of " Beauty " with the word
Glory in our translations. It is a far more appropriate
word for the object of æsthetic experience in the case
of any one living in the East, I should think. I was
constantly being penetrated by the experiences of the
eyes when I was in Egypt. But a beautiful land is
not exactly what you would call it. The rising and
the setting of the sun are too tremendous to be called
beautiful. " The Heavens declare the glory of God."

" Thou that makest the outgoings of the morning
and evening to praise Thee."

And the noonday does not reveal beauties of shape
and colour, but there is just a radiance of light and
richness of shadow, an aerial splendour which is exactly
a glory.

I have embarked on an interesting experiment

lately. I got some of the leading spirits among the men together, and read them a paper I had written for the occasion on the value of the forces of the unseen world in everyday life. Afterwards they talked quite freely, and it is proposed to repeat the venture, they bringing some of their friends perhaps. I am writing a paper on Prayer to read to them.

It was on the whole a great success, the first meeting, and I had the sense of doing something extremely valuable to myself and almost certainly useful to them.

To E. P.

December 10th, 1916.

We can from another point of view see the necessity for transcending our judgments of life as good and evil. After all, without evil there is no good. To think that by removing evil you reach good is absurd. We could not live for more than a day or so were it not for the pain of hunger and thirst which forces us to nourish ourselves. Security from danger is no good except in so far as the ordinary accidents of life are evil, and peace of mind is only a good in so far as the questionings and strivings of mind are evil. All efforts to make a heaven of human goods end in absurd scenes with crowns and harps and so forth. At the same time we cannot rest content with a world constituted thus. Such relativity is intolerable. We inevitably seek an absolute. Can we not find it in Truth, Beauty, and Love, and was not this Christ's message ? Truth needs no falsehood, Beauty no blemish, Love no hate to make them true, beautiful, and tender, and what else did Christ value but sincerity, grace, and tenderness in every moment of life ? I think St. Paul is, on the whole, true to Him, though the servant is not greater than his Lord.

As you say, he accepts the goods and evils of life, and does not demand that goods should be sacrificed or evils self-imposed, but he welcomes life as it comes that he may as it were climb over its limitations and contrasts into the fuller land of liberty, " where there is neither Jew nor Greek, circumcision nor uncircumcision, barbarian, Scythian, bond or free, but Christ is all in all." And now abideth Faith, Hope, and Charity—these three; and are they not the conviction of Truth, the hope of perfect beauty, and the love " which seeketh not her own" ?

To R. G. B.

February 1917.

. . . One way and another these times are bringing men back to God—are they not ?

I have had some interesting and precious hours with my men, and found them very willing to listen to what I had to urge upon them.

These have now just left, going before me to the M.G. Corps. I miss them greatly—for our thinking together of the deep things of God has made a very happy relation between us in our daily work, giving even in the alienation of our military ranks a new value for one another, which I felt greatly added to our efficiency.

We talk a great deal these days about building a better world from out the wreck of the past, but we need more boldly to proclaim the true foundation, the link between man and man which has no flaw, reverence for one another, for God is in us all—calm and cheer in our hearts because our lives are in His hands—" He in us and we in Him." I take that to be the centre of the revelation of Christ, the cornerstone of a happier temple of life.

ALGERNON HYDE VILLIERS

HARROWBY CAMP, GRANTHAM.
May 6th, 1917.

I have arrived very safely, and find myself in a rather minute cubicle copiously adorned with pictures from the papers of ladies more or less undressed.

I found Temple's *Mens Creatrix* the most excellent reading, and the time in the train seemed very short.

I was glad to find a sentence in Temple of how we have to play our parts in life in a " surround " of almost all but complete ignorance. I feel that so strongly. " Lighten our darkness " is a universal sort of prayer. That reminds me that I went into St. Pancras Church and heard a very war-time curate gabbling through the great charge to Joshua as if he were reading an Act of Parliament. The choir was good and I enjoyed singing the Te Deum.

May 11th.

One feels quite like being in a tunnel here, taken up with the minute study of the things they teach, and lost to the world for the next few weeks. The end of the tunnel is only a tiny spot in the distance, but one knows it means liberation.

Human nature, however, can never be eliminated, even by a machine-gun course, and there was a mess meeting last night which was very entertaining. The President, a very nice fellow evidently, while assuring us that this was the only mess in the camp worth considering at all, yet felt obliged to call this meeting and warn the members of this social paradise against insulting the waitresses and pouring their drinks into the piano ! . . .

I have just been having an absorbing discussion on the position of the black races with an ex-officer of a West Indian regiment, and a student of Glasgow

University who honours the H.L.I. The former was very interesting, the latter very loquacious. . . .

May 12th.

I set out after luncheon by way of the town, and went out of it westwards towards Melton for a mile or two till I came to a place called Harlaxton. . . . Here I found a village of wonderful cottages with the quaintest porches of wood and wooden crowned gables on the brick walls. Such a jumble of dear little buildings and unexpected courts and archways you never saw.

It lies just off the road, and almost prevents any access to the fine church, well cared for and graceful with a clerestory and spire. . . .

Then I came out on to a great plateau of sweeping fields with splendid views to the north and west. It is a fine country indeed, real agricultural and much nearer than Sussex to the French feeling. The hedge-rows were lovely and full of white-throats. . . . There is no question here of listening for warblers. White-throats, blackcaps, and tree-pippits simply shout at one all the time. The air rings with larks, and every group of trees is pealing with blackbirds. . . . Beyond Ponton I got into a regular downs' valley, deep grass slopes on either side. When I came out at the top of this the country began to roll out in fine style, and a little farther north (I was beginning to work home-wards) I came to a great open cross-roads and the sense of high Lincolnshire fairly overtook me. It certainly is grand to see the wide roads with their generous verges, and the great fenced fields flat on every hand. Not even a distant air-station could spoil the " high " feeling. What a good word that is so used ! The sun was gone and the vast sky-scene was every exquisite shade of grey. It was thrilling.

There is a solemnity about a great dull landscape
which no work of man quite rivals. No doubt it is
partly, or largely, the sky-scape that produces so much
effect, but Lincolnshire is fit to lie under a wide
expanse of sky.

I was now getting to the country which lies immediately above this camp which is east of Grantham town.
I found a picturesque derelict inn on Ermine Street,
and there I had some tea and made a sketch. . . .

So I pitched down off the heights and the still solitudes into the valley and the hideous hutted camps—
rather sad. Then it began to rain, and I took refuge
with my sketch when I got in.

May 25th.

So far I have two firsts. This afternoon we have
another exam. in gun drill.

I have been thinking of the relation of these little
efforts to my prayers, and trying to express the
reconciliation which I feel between the thought that
God will not exactly cause one to get first-class marks,
and the sense that it does make all the difference
whether or no we share such small worldly things with
Him. The difference made must, it seems to me,
touch not only our own feelings about these things,
but also our actual power of doing them well, or at
any rate better than we otherwise would. For if the
former only held good, it would reduce one to an
attitude of indifference to effectiveness in the daily
round which amounts to paralysis. If we literally
don't care what happens, there is no reason for trying,
is there ? The reconciliation comes, I think, in the
idea of God as a real Person not wholly unlike a
human being who loves us and whom we love. Thus
He is at once a pure incentive to effort leading to
effectiveness, and a consolation by the proportion of His

great gift of the power of communion with Himself to the transitory character of our immediate strivings. That quite extraordinary gift is being given to me in greater fullness as time goes on, allowing of course for ups and downs depending *apparently* upon health and environment, and so on. For instance, when I am feeling bored at a lecture, as I was this morning, there will sometimes reach me just the recollection of God with the most cheering effect. We think far too exclusively of God and religion enforcing things upon us, requiring things of us, and so we just throw away the happiness of His friendship. Other forms of happiness cheer us with the remembrance of them, but this one, I fancy, will never cloy for one thing, and, for another, can never be out of our grasp. " Who shall separate us from the love of Christ ? "

It is because of this unique goodness for life in the realised relation of God and man that it is so important for us to find that way of access to the Divine along which we really find Him as a friend we can truly enjoy. This is the essential liberty of the Sons of God to which we so hesitate to trust ourselves. We are all children of His alike, but also each in his or her own way. Don't you think that people imagine that God only cares for a certain type of character—shall we say as like Jesus' as possible ?—and forget that we insult God by supposing Him to prefer a copy, however good, to an original ? The life of Jesus is not a pattern (as some people have tried to make it quite literally, haven't they ?), but an inspiration to move us by its power in the present moment towards the great end of God's children for which we were made, the taking, that is, of a fuller and fuller share in the life of His family or Kingdom.

What a sermon !

To V. V.

May 20th, 1917.

I went to Lincoln yesterday.

It is a mighty cathedral, and the Whitsun service was profoundly beautiful and blessed. The splendid clothes of bishop and clergy, the simple music sailing away down the glorious flights of columns and arches, and the exquisite old windows glowing like fields of flowers in Paradise made a memorable setting for the worship of God.

The service was, as it should be everywhere, the central one. God's own institution has gathered round it the very kernel of living faith, and in a tin hut in camp here, or among the splendours of Lincoln Cathedral, I find His promise fulfilled: Where two or three are gathered together——

HARROWBY CAMP.
May 29th, 1917.

I am sorry to hear of all the vexations you were caused. . . .

It is the most wretched thing to feel alienated from God, for it means a contradiction in one's own soul which is the gist of unhappiness. One longs to be at one with oneself, and at peace with Him, and it seems so hard that the other law should be working in us, which we would so gladly expel but cannot. It is a mystery, but I expect that progressively Christ can, and will, lead us out of the maze. So one must never despair of oneself or Him, but make the most of our best moments, enjoying them, realising how much best they are, and how un- natural, in a sense, is everything which is out of 'tune with them and which obscures the truth in them revealed.

This is a nice little mess and a man is playing Gilbert and Sullivan awfully well, to my great consolation. There has not been a draft of officers for some weeks,[1] and they expect to be sending one soon, so I dare say I shall not be here long. . . .

The perfect smoothness and happiness of my morning, and the kindly, generous attitude I have found everywhere, seem clearly to flow from my half-hour of close communion with the Unseen and Eternal before I set out on my round of office calls, and I look forward with something like enthusiasm to the far greater and more searching trials which lie before my spirit, absolutely sure that the Key to every difficulty is in His hands Who is able to do exceedingly abundantly above all that we ask and think, and wondering and hoping if perhaps I may live to say with St. Paul, "Now thanks be to God our Father, Who always maketh us to triumph in Christ Jesus our Lord." Think of me as trying day by day (for simple sense's sake and because it seems so plainly the thing to do) to rely more and more on the power that can never fail to be true to itself, and on the love from which neither life nor death nor any other creature can separate us.

If I should die in France—let us face this once and for all—you must think that God led me that way, and remember that to go when one is most keenly alive to God's Being is surely a great blessing. I will not for an instant seek such an end, because I love to live with you. Yet, if it is so to be, you surely will not sorrow as those who have no hope, for I have proved

[1] He had asked to have his name put down for the next.

and know that a human soul in its real nature, when
it is most composed and serene, most truly undis-
turbedly itself, passes out beyond life and death, and
has its place in the fullness of Him Who filleth all
in all.

LETTERS FROM FRANCE

VERY leisurely we proceed on our way to
Camiers. The crossing was smoothness itself, and the approach to Boulogne of our
little flotilla, three Channel boats and two escorting
torpedo-boats, was a beautiful scene. The monument
on the down top—it is Napoleon and his camp that it
commemorates, I think—is just what the French can,
and we cannot, achieve. It has a minaret-like air,
with its soaring, slender column, and the cupola effect
of the pedestal for the statue, which tops the whole
without the common look of toppling off! I enjoyed
the sense of being in France, and the vehement energy
of our young one-eyed porter, who slung our *two*
valises over his shoulder and went reeling away with
them to the motor-lorry—grommelant et bougonnant
in an inarticulate but to me wholly delightful fashion.
B. and I sailed serenely through the harum-scarum of
the quay-swarms of soldiers, Major-Generals, military
landing officers, Staff-Captains, and A.S.C. drivers,
all sorting themselves with the utmost quiet and calm,
but wholly without direction—a triumph of good
organisation really, but full of pleasing disinvolture
to the unaccustomed eye. We formed an M.G. party
and rumbled away up the most precipitous slopes to

63

this camp, where " reinforcing officers " spend the
night.

An admirable young Scotsman seems to be in charge
of the camp. A Second-Lieutenant with a most tiresome job, he wears his Balmoral on one ear with
unruffled jauntiness, and in cooing accents explains
to a fresh batch of officers of all ranks each night that
they are confined to camp, will sleep six in a tent, and
that there will be some tea at 9 p.m. in yon hut (where
I now write). " Tea " was inimitable, and took me
straight back to August 1914. The Salvation ladies
rating everybody up hill and down, and the same old
jam on which I lived at Culford, and the same old tea
I learned to drink at Abbassia, and after-thoughts of
tinned salmon, and the sense of irresponsible picnicking
which can never be arranged, but is so acutely enjoy-
able when one drops into it. . . .

OFFICERS' CLUB, ETAPLES.
July 30th.

Active service at the back of the front is a perfect
picnic so far. We have had the day to go into Étaples,
and arrange about pay-books, etc., which took two
minutes, and we have found a most excellent club
here, where we had luncheon, and are just going to
have dinner. The afternoon was spent on a visit to
Paris Plage. The tramway went through nice Corot
woods to the cheerful little collection of laughably
dodgy houselets which constitute P.P. Even the rain
could not make the expedition a failure. We had the
most excellent tea—not the equal of the Veuve
Devasour at Chamonix, where alone peach ices blossom,
but still very light and delicious. The place is swarm-
ing with soldiers—the coast a camp simply. We saw
some 6-mm. guns rolling on their railway-cars, camou-
flaged like giraffes. I have applied for leave to go to
Havre, and the Adjutant was by no means discouraging.

64

Everywhere the utmost bonhomie and cheerfulness are conspicuous. . . .

The downs behind the camp at Camiers are very jolly; quite like Wiltshire, and I expect if it clears they will be sketched before long.

> A.P.O. S. 18.
> *July 31st.*

It is another rough, dark day, but most luckily our tent is watertight, and my position out of reach of the small stream that inevitably comes in at the door. We walked home some four miles last night in heavy rain. . . .

Our outing of yesterday was really great fun. Joffre [1] appeared at the tent door this morning, and we trysted for the afternoon. I have just come back from a walk with him, and tea at a sort of an ancient bungalow business, looking out on a lake, surrounded by fir-clad sandhills, exactly like a bit of Surrey—say Frensham Pond—where Conrad once saw nine different ducks, or something equally fantastic. He seems to have had some imperial ructions with his flock, but to be in good spirits generally. We had a good lecture on Vimy to-day, and should have done some revolver if it had not poured with rain. I read my favourite Ps. cvii. for the thirty-first this morning.

> A.P.O. S. 18
> *August 4th.*

Yet another twenty-four hours of delay. I am not sorry, for I hope it will just make the series of your letters go on reaching me without a break, and also because it does at last seem possible that the rain is going to stop, so that I shall travel the better, and find things partially dried up when I arrive. . . . I must

[1] Captain Robert Jeffrey

tell you that the Osterhove Camp has only quite recently been made a necessity for reinforcing officers, and the very primitive arrangements were of an improvised order. We mess much better here. The anteroom, however, is most deplorable. There is nothing to sit on, because the officers have broken the chairs to pieces at such a rate that the Mess President refuses to buy any more. J.'s hut, with tables and chairs, is a perfect boon. We have had no parades this morning, so I have had an interesting hour studying a W.O. pamphlet and reading Smuts's fine speech at the Parliamentary dinner. What a fine man he must be! It is water in the desert to read such a speech, with so much penetration and spiritual force.

Don't you think this of Pascal is fine?—"God puts religion into the mind by its reasonableness, and into the heart by grace."

Intellectual honesty and thoroughness are absolutely part of Christian living, and grow, so I hope and believe, more and more possible as we try so to live. "The testimony of the Lord is sure, and giveth wisdom unto the simple," as we read this morning.

In St. Luke I read the chapter that begins with the Lord's Prayer. The woes of the Pharisees are strangely little different from ours, aren't they? I thought they fell upon our well-meaning, trumpery English life, both public and private, while the last verse rips open the emptiness of it all with terrible precision. But the fact that Christ's piercing criticisms were made of a section only of His contemporaries reminds one that there are, in all probability, far more people who have not forsaken judgment, and the love of God, nor allowed themselves to be given to the folly of ambition and vanity, than we commonly suppose. "Judgment" here means discernment, I take it—a true estimate of life's values. One cannot suppose that, taken together, human life is all as pathetically

66

beside the mark as a forgotten grave, though such a description has only too much applicability to any individual life.

I think it is quite certain that I get off to-morrow morning. It is a good thing, as I have had enough of waiting here. The clear-up makes possible a demonstration of the new barrage work, which I am glad not to be going to miss.

Péronne, Officers' Club.
August 5th.

Before trying to describe what to me has been an intensely interesting afternoon, I must tell you that I spend to-night here, and go up to the company to-morrow morning. They are in the trenches, which they tell me are " Luxe, calme "—though " volupté " would be slightly overdoing it, I suppose.

Well, now for the famous scenes I have just passed through. The first signal of the war zone was a distant sight of Albert tower, with the drooping Madonna, and then we entered a fine rolling country very wide and bare, and the clumps of trees began to look a bit battered. As we went on the land became a wilderness—nothing to indicate the presence of man, as we are accustomed to recognise it. There are no divisions between fields in this region, and cultivation having ceased, the ground is covered with wild grass, and flowers—sheets of keck, and patches of poppies, loose-strife, and that coarse yellow flower that flourishes in every forsaken plot of ground. One can see that there were once woods here and there, but nothing but a few bare stumps remain, and they do not the least break the sense of smooth annihilation—the blotted-out look of the land. In the distance I could see the soft, furry brown slopes, just picked out with white, where I suppose trenches had been, but close at hand one does not notice them. The wild-flowers

67

have mastered them already. In one or two places
one can imagine what was a village. Perhaps one
house-corner suggests it—the only thing standing;
and then one can see a few foundations, otherwise—
blank. Every western side of a ridge—we seemed to
pass several a few hundred yards or so long, shows
the neglected rubbish of a whole soldier colony,
punctuated in its dirty white clothes, with the little
black doorway leading to the dug-outs. There was
not a living creature to be seen but a couple of magpies
and a couple of rooks. The river has the appearance
of a great marsh, most beautifully still and mysterious,
a broken wooden trestle-bridge in front, and the
low ridge flat against the sky on the other side—such
a sketch! It was a lovely afternoon, breathless, and
violet skies to the east, with a luminous western heaven.
Who has described the scene in verses we know well?
"Where no birds sing." Even more than of the
downs, Robert Bridges might have said of these
valleys, "O still solitudes, only matched in the skies."

Even the touching groups of graves could not make
the scene pathetic; it was too fine a burial-ground for
sadness, where the brave bodies lie, crowning as it
were the dead landscape with deep loneliness, and
undisturbed or intruded upon by any but their passing
comrades. We were then in a truck—the familiar
Hommes 40, Chevaux 8, and everybody was very
silent.

One little Captain sat looking too wretched for
words, and an Indian Lancer officer seemed to shrivel
up more and more as we went on. Near me an N.F.
Captain was very determined to enjoy Mrs. Proudie's
reception in *Barchester Towers*. But he didn't seem
to get on very well with it, moving his finger across
the page to keep himself up to it, as I used to do with
Cicero or Demosthenes.

We got here, and some went straight into the town.

With a melancholy infantry Second Lieutenant, of perhaps some forty summers, I went up to the camp, had tea, picked my tent and disposed of my belongings. "East Surrey" gradually cheered up. Perhaps he was encouraged by my irrepressible zest for everything. The camp much better than Osterhove—no Salvationists—was America all over, just perching, untidily, like a missel-thrush's nest, on the famous high ground above the town.

After tea we came down here, "E. S." becoming quite communicative, and less anxious to remind me of how soon I should hate every sight and sound of France. We both thought the town had not been much knocked about, but there is not a building intact. Félix Potin—the ubiquitous—keeps his nameboard leaning, but legible. The road has been repaired—a fine, wide street like Dunbar, narrowing at either end—and the houses simply heaps of rubbish. The church is a ruin. It must have been fine, to judge from what remains of the west front, and a few windows. The place is uninhabited, of course—another striking novelty for me—and gives one a sense of the utmost pitifulness. It has no flowers to hide its abject state, its forlorn desertion, but just hangs its poor head, done for, *halas*.[1] Whether this house was spared, or escaped, I don't know, but it is very handsome, and little damaged. There is a great deal of good decoration about the panellings, and the rooms look over a little terraced garden to the river, and another stretch of soft, smooth vacancy. It is a pleasant, characteristic place, wonderfully welcome after the miserable mess-huts at Camiers.

"E. S." and I are going to dine here.

[1] Arabic for "finished."

ALGERNON HYDE VILLIERS

This is the most lovely morning, the summer fairly
come back to us. Would you believe it? we don't go
on until 1.45, so I am going to try and make a sketch
away down by the river, if I can get there.

I have had the most comfortable night on a wood
and wire bedstead of luxurious design. I like this
camp, and last night I was able to get a regular bath,
in a balmy moonlight which was quite romantic, while
this morning damp things are getting thoroughly dry.

I must tell you that as we were sitting down to
dinner last night, the reader of *Barchester Towers* came
along unaccompanied, so as I liked his looks, and was
not too much thrilled by " East Surrey," I beckoned
him to our table.

He proved a most charming and guileless child.
He has commanded a company of a notably rough
battalion for over a year, and is now only twenty-three.
He told us all his affairs. He is a wholesale fruiterer,
and vastly proud of his business. His love-affairs and
his disputes with his seniors were all related. He proved
a capital sauce to our good dinner, and it is really
wonderful to think of one so juvenile in every way
having such a position. We are a great people undoubtedly.

August 7th.

It seems ages since I last wrote to you, though it
was only yesterday morning, but the critical moment
of passing into the war zone puts a great gulf between
past and present. I must tell you all about it. We
left the rest-camp and bumbled along on a little trolly-
line for some time in the early afternoon. Then I
found the transport, and waited some ages for the
return of the transport officer. He was a jolly, cheery
fellow, and with his aid I reorganised my kit for the

trenches. His wagons started, and we sat down to an excellent dinner. Then, mounted on a bold, black light draft horse, I set out in pursuit with him. So I rode to the war after all! and a jolly good ride it was. We went fast at first, while it was still pretty light, and caught up the teams halted with others under the brow of a ridge. When the light was gone we crossed it, and I nearly jumped out of the saddle when a big battery, no distance away, suddenly banged off a burst. I love the roar and sighing of the shells, and the sense of incredible velocity which the sound of their passage conveys. From this sentiment you will collect that we do not have too much of such music!

To-day I have walked many miles, and visited numerous tiny little nests of destruction for the Boche. Soon I shall be in charge of one. For the present I remain at Company Headquarters, where we do excellently well. The dug-outs are not dark or stuffy, and I feel thoroughly at home. The one blow is a kindly but preposterous being—a sort of buckram Mr. Jingle, full of gas, and bluff, and oaths, and stupidity —most tiresome. . . .

To-night I shall go out firing, I expect, and so the days will fly away, full of novelties and human interest. I wish I could think of you as well off as I am. The Company has been in for thirty-seven days, and expect soon to get a short reprieve. They go down one by one to have a bath in a fairly distant village. The weather is misty and hot. I have not seen a paper since Sunday. Poor Kerensky—what a dreadful plunging into the abyss it all is!

August 8th.

We had quite an amusing time of it last night. All went well, and I was back here by 12.30, and had a good sleep this morning. At one moment the artillery

71

did what they are pleased to call a concentration.
In other words, they made the air blue for a few
moments. They were going plumb over our heads,
and, added to our own four guns, the din was
terrific. What it must be like to live in that condition
of atmosphere for weeks, I simply cannot imagine.
There must be moments of pause, of course, but they
say the racket is more continuous than one could
conceive possible. On a small scale it was simply a
new thrill. I have spent the day going round with
the C.O. . . . and enjoying it all immensely. . . .
There has been tremendous rain this evening, and the
mess dug-out is a huge puddle.

August 9th.

Those days—July 30th to August 2nd—certainly
were dreadful, but it is splendid that we did not fail
to achieve something substantial, in spite of the awful
rain. Now I must take up the question of God, the
Psalms, and the weather. I can, of course, only give
you the effect upon my mind of my own experience,
and I don't lose sight of the fact that every one has
got to find these things for himself. Still, I should
like to think that you would try and see it my way.

I don't think God is on either side in the sense in
which I am on one side and a given Boche on the
other. Again, I don't think it less absurd to blame
or charge Him with the weather than Lucian did,
when he described that cart-load of hail for Cappadocia.
The root of the thing is that His ways are not as our
ways, but that our ways might become something like,
or in conformity with, His, only we won't have it so.
God is a Spirit, and speaks primarily to the spirit of
man which is listening for His voice. The reactions
of a human spirit, which has allowed God to possess
it, upon its so-called material surroundings, would
probably, in fact I think certainly, rob them of their

cruelty and provocation, but that does not mean that they would be altered. Why God does not arrange the rainfall like the sunrise is not our affair; but if we choose to have a war on, it can hardly be said that He is against us because the rain spoils our offensive. . . .

Then as regards the praise of God in the Psalms, how can praise of Him ever be " excessive " ?

For praise is not flattery; it is acclamation, being possessed by God, and lifted by Him into the sunlight of His presence. You cannot have too much of that; for it is just exactly that which carries us to victory over circumstances, and which we need most when things look blackest. So it has always been, I think, down the history of the saints. At the time of their trial, in prisons and tortures and lions' dens, and at all times of anguish, they have praised God because in so doing they came nearest to Him, and felt His strength sufficient for them.

If you reject this view, where are you to turn in hours of anguish ? " Master, to whom shall we go ? " " Whom have I in heaven but Thee, and there is none upon earth that I desire in comparison with Thee."

I think when Christ says hard things about hating father and mother, and let the dead bury their dead, he conveys that there are times when neither human relations nor a sense of duty can save us from misery, weakness, and the spoiling of our lives, but that God always can, so that there is no earthly claim so essential as His claim to our thoughts and wills. " My peace I give unto you," *but " not as the world giveth* give I unto you." Not as the *world* giveth, that's the point. Don't look for God's action in the same direction as you would for a man's. He belongs to another order of peace and power and fullness to us, but He will come and be with us if we could only manage to let Him in, if we only could see the things that belong to our peace.

I feel it hard, just as perhaps you do, to keep looking in the right direction. . . . I build fancies of ambition, but I know very well that my real happiness is not made up of getting on, and being rewarded or acknowledged by men, but in the simple thought of my destiny being guided by Him. When I feel clear on that point, then I am not worried, or anxious about success, or failure, or recognition, then I always enjoy the sense of triumph through my tiny atom of love for Him leading me to the marvellous hem of His garment.

August 10th.

I had to stop short yesterday in writing to you, for which I was sorry. I know you don't like all-sermon letters—quite right too, but the Major was ready to go. He took me off to my post, and I began to settle down by myself in a cellar, with a very picturesque painted figure of the Madonna standing on a table.

The church must have been near, but I can't recognise it. However I was turned out later in the evening, and settled in here with some jolly infantry boys, with whom my guns co-operate, and whose telephone I can use to get through to Company Headquarters. Now I am properly in the saddle my days are rather like a journalist's. I am up all night, and sleep till about 2 o'clock in the afternoon. I don't mind it at all, though it was beastly wet and sticky last night. Now it is a lovely clear night and a pleasure to be out in the dark. I have a nice orderly, who always goes with me wherever I go, so that if I were hit I should not lie helpless. He wrote such a nice letter to his wife to-day, which I censored, about their praying for one another.

The teams which I look after want a little brisking up, in small ways, but seem to be most excellent fellows. I wish I saw more of them. If ever we go out of the line I shall get to know them better.

I liked the article on " prayer." It is a little vague, and to my mind that is a little unfortunate on a subject of such importance that clarity is essential. " Lord, teach us how to pray," was a most sensible prayer, wasn't it ? and one does want to work out one's own method with the greatest care and honesty.

Well-meant humbug was our Lord's peculiar aversion, and though the *well*-meaning is a great set-off to the humbug, greater than in His time because better *meant*, still humbug defeats itself, and must do so, whether He condemns it or no. That's just how Christ's teaching often strikes me. He taught, not some fancy of His own, but the principles on which the world is run in any case, but taught them in such a way that we get from Him, better than from elsewhere, the cue to our part, and light on our darkness about ultimate things.

It is 3 a.m., and the others are turning in. I have to go round at 3.45, and am going to do my read now when all is quiet. I have finished Luke xv— beautiful tales and the *un*prodigal son so full of meaning. But I love chapter x, the good Samaritan, and Mary and Martha—one of the most vivid, touching episodes in the Gospels, I think. Good morning.

August 11th.

Don't be alarmed at my account of Boche projectiles. He never hits anybody, and only does it to annoy, because he thinks it teases. We of course do the same, only more of it. Countess B.'s news is interesting. I am glad to hear of the old régime not regretted, for treachery is even worse than the crazy folly with which poor Kerensky has to struggle. What a reed in the storm he seems.

In reading about the mammon of unrighteousness last night, I felt quite sure the verse about making friends with it is satirical. The close of the passage is very suggestive, isn't it ?—" Who shall give you that which is your own ? "

August 12th.

We are in for a noisy night to-night, as some neighbours of ours are getting busy. To-morrow I shall be able to tell you all about it.

Meantime I am rather tired. My new landlords made a lot of noise getting up, and disturbed my slumbers. I don't like them half as much as their predecessors. The night after to-morrow I go to another place near by, which I hear is very well found.

August 13th.

There was not much of a concert last night, and the choir left the orchestra in the lurch somewhere or other, so that nothing came of it. The performance is doing again now. I have just come in from listening to the overture. It was rather splendid, but nothing overwhelming.

I was truly distressed to see beloved Esmond's [1] death. Those people who contribute so much to life by just being delightful are the most painful losses. Esmond will be passionately mourned at Amisfield, and elsewhere. Poor Colonel, I am sorry to think how wretched he will be about it.

August 14th.

Now I am writing from my new quarters—a proper subterranean affair.

It has been a great night, pitch dark, and slippery as the devil, and I have got fairly plastered with mud. However, in spite of difficulties, all has been got happily done, and I have been wonderfully kept up in my floundering struggles by the thought of Christ in the

---

[1] The Hon. Esmond Elliot. *Lt, 2ᵈ Bn Scots Guards † 6 August near Ypres*

storm—Why are ye fearful ? I have had some trouble with an N.C.O., but I expect I shall get him right if he doesn't do anything too hopeless in the meantime. The other one is a fine fellow with a D.C.M. He won it near Loos for rescuing a gun out of a bust-up position in the middle of a " straf," when all the team proper had been knocked out. . .. .

I made the acquaintance of the General to-day. Everybody says he is exactly like me to look at. Anyhow, he seems a fine fellow ! ! ! I had a pleasant, brief impression of him. . . .

August 15th.

To-day I must tell you I went to an observation post and saw my first free Boche. He was a funny-looking old thing, and toddled across the picture in a very unwarlike fashion. I dare say he was a cook. Then I saw a sentry with his helmet, a sort of bluish colour. But what made me most jealous of the Boche is the pleasant landscape in which he lives. I saw big fields all stooked and ready to be carried, and then happy church spires still quite intact. It was quite a surprise, which shows how quickly one gets accustomed even to such unfamiliar things as my battered village.[1] There is not anything approaching an entire house left—a bit of wall here and a dangling roof there is about all. I notice that there are no farms among the fields here. The farms and farm buildings of a neighbourhood evidently concentrate themselves into a village, and work the land from it. Thus one gets a lot of what were quite big villages (with traces of very substantial buildings), but no ruins between one of them and another. "Well, dear" (as the men say in their nice letters), " I don't think I've anything more to say at present, so will close."

[1] Gonnelieu.

77

The presence of God always with one is a great comfort and joy. So when I lie down to sleep, or have times of waiting or weariness, I am linked to all I love best, and most enjoy, by the thought of God—the act of looking His way, which is the same act here, there and all the world over. I hope you understand how natural and inevitable, and not at all artificial, this is ? I begin to believe that all the great phrases of religious experience, which have in the past seemed wonderful, but beyond my literal comprehension, are really true in quite a simple way, and require no great or special endowment, or temperament, for us to realise them in common life. "Lo, I am with you alway," which you love so much, and, "I will not leave you comfortless, I will come to you," and "Who shall separate us from the love of Christ ? "—all these so prodigious in a way are, I think, fulfilled in quite a simple fashion, though none the less a glorious one. But I begin to wish one could see God face to face in some way, and talk directly to Him. . . . Life will have more of one than a perpetual delicious walk across the links. There is no escape from that. We cannot be happy on that plane indefinitely. So there come effort and sacrifice and sadness, to make up the fullness of life, to give us a larger share in the Divine nature, and so constitute our only true and lasting joy. As Christ said to the sons of Zebedee, "Ye know not what spirit ye are of." Although it is in a sense ours, we do not know the Divine nature in anything like its fullness. We recognise its outline in Christ, and for the rest we must trust God to be in us, as He was in Him "through all the changing scenes of life, its trouble and its joy."

It is puzzling to know how far it is up to us to seek God, since what we want is to be found of him—"not having our *own* nature," as St. Paul says. Practically, however, there appears to be no difficulty. For the act of looking His way is itself inspired by Him. Pascal's greatest phrase is: "Be comforted; thou wouldst not seek me if thou hadst not found me."

Another sermon, but a cheerful one, I hope.

All goes well here, and after to-morrow night I shall go back where I was before, and be glad of the change from this mole's existence.

August 17th.

No, I never see a Frenchman of any sort, and hardly a French word. The horrible Germans even renamed the streets—Haupt Strasse, Schloss Strasse, and Juden Gasse one reads, and on what were evidently the best houses Offz. Qu., very black and clear. . . .

We have had two exquisite days and nights, in which the country here has had a lovely look of its own. You know the effect of *width* one gets so much in French landscapes. The skies have been filled with creamy gleaming clouds, and all the colour has been in them above the brownish green ground. I have explored the pathetic little village. One farm we should have loved. It was just the right mixture, I should say, between mansion and workplace. In the dwelling-house the hat-rack remains conspicuously intact, among the ruin of walls and ceilings and roofs. There is never one stick of furniture. Outside the creepers were bushing out all over the crumbled walls. Near by there stands quite a château, with a mansarde window still leaning precariously out of the smashed tile roof.

August 19th.

I wish I could tell you how happy and well I feel, what a different man, for the change from subterranean gropings to the light of heaven. The nights, I think, make the greatest difference—or rather, I should say, the hours devoted to sleep. In a deep dug-out one

wakes up like an underdone bun, and though I did not
sleep heavily, this morning I feel thoroughly refreshed.
The air was free to come in six inches from my nose,
and there is a draught clean through the shelter.
Then a bath in a half-tub filled with rain-water and a
thorough inspection of my clothes was greatly cheering.
. . . Now, instead of a chilly, stuffy, one-candle-lighted
den, I am at ease in a sandbag and steel shelter, with
bright sunshine pouring into it. The lack of air, and
the unnecessarily bad messing of my late hosts, had
quite upset my interior economy . . . but all that
has gone and I have enjoyed an excellent luncheon,
with salad and stewed plums and delicious biscuits.
In the dug-out we had tea and coffee *mixed* one day,
and on another occasion the tea was made in a tin half
full of *disinfectant*. In a deep dug-out the dark makes
it very hard for the cooks, and nothing tastes right in
that stale atmosphere. It is curious, too, how chilly it
gets down there in the small hours. It must be *horrible*
in winter. I did my level best not to think of these
things when I was there, and insisted with myself that
I must be glad to share, in a trifling measure, the
discomforts of which thousands had had months, and
even years, to put up with. Having managed to get
through my first such spell, " superasque evadere ad
auras," I expect subsequent descents will be much
easier. We carried on with four guns from 11.30 to
2.30 last night, supporting an operation of a minor
character, which turned out quite well.

During the night there were some glorious big
bombardments to either side of us, splendid to watch,
and really prodigious to think of in relation to our
position of two years ago, in the matter of artillery.
Our own firing was interesting. The guns did very
well. They need careful supplying on 'such occasions, and I thought that should have been better
organised.

August 21st.

The Boche posted in No Man's Land last night a long news-sheet in favour of peace, written in admirable English. It purported to give the views of an eminent Russian statesman to the effect that instant peace was a necessity for Russia if she would avoid complete prostration. The sublime strategic developments of the march of the German armies in Galicia was enlarged upon. In a final paragraph the enmity of England to peace was discussed in a hopeful tone. Her great expansion and power were set down to her far-sighted policy, and her readiness to use blood and iron. I wonder what purpose they thought all this would serve ?

August 21st.

I appreciate the force of all you say about my sermon on God, the war, and the weather, very keenly. I am quite off the mark where I seem to convey that God is an invisible King, Who knows nothing of our wars, and of Whom we can know nothing. I did not mean to suggest that, and I quite agree with you that we are taught by Christ to lay all our lives and interests before God. But I suggest that we are wrong if we do so with our minds already made up as to how those lives should be directed and those interests satisfied. That seems to fore-doom our prayers to ineffectiveness, for the essence of prayer is the receiving of new light and vision from God on the things which are weighing upon us.

Again, I think we are wrong and unwise, asking for disappointment, if we ask God to stop the war, as we imagine the Kaiser could, by a *coup de main*. Broadly speaking, His way is to do things through us, not for us. That was why it was a temptation to Christ to command the stones to be made bread. At the same time I strongly agree that the Kingdom of God belongs

c   81

here and now. In any heart wherein God is King
there is a mighty power to mould the world for good.
Christ Himself is the supreme example, and it is very
noticeable that the Kingdom of God in Him has been
manifested, not nearly so much by the mighty works
which He performed among His contemporaries, as
by the influencing of millions of lives, through the
handful of friends whose love for Him on earth transformed their lives. He worked primarily through men,
not for them. He always attributes His miracles to
the spiritual condition He has produced in the people
helped. "Thy faith hath saved thee"—not "my
external power." What you say about praise is just
what I feel. It is in the dark hour that it is most
appropriate. I wish I could sum it all up. . . .

Surely I am thoroughly normal and commonplace.
That used to be said to be my characteristic.

It was so said by the President of Magdalen to
Pollock about my demyship, and the latter, in handing
it on, said, "What better endowment for the service
of God and of men ? " And in this business of turning
to God, I don't think I have any ecstatic or *exalté* strain.
I think the best sense is contained in the Bible, and that
the effort to seek to follow Christ, at however great a
distance, is the most sensible thing a man can do.
"Master, to whom shall we go ? " His life was
centred upon the thought of God. He and His
Father were one. Such perfection is our unattainable
goal, but as we strive towards it, real happiness comes.
The more often we remember the name of the Lord
our God each day, the stronger and happier we become.
So we may begin to love Him for the happiness which
comes from the thought of Him, and as we slowly grow
in that wonderful human capacity—that of loving God
—our whole nature falls into harmony ; we may hope
to rise higher and higher above the transitory things
of this life, and so reach to the heart of the human and

divine enigma, that our days may be fulfilled with God's grace and heavenly benediction, and pass imperceptibly into that fullness of time and place, which is ever with the Lord.

So it seems to me plainly worth while, and supremely worth while, to try and receive into our souls the message God has to give us, and that is what I mean by prayer, and praise, and study, and meditation—the search for that true and perfect way that leadeth unto life.

I must stop now. I have some interesting work to do, and, asking God not to leave me to do it without His inner guidance, I must set about it. My section is coming together, and everything looks very promising. I cannot help seeing God's hand in all the events of these days. How easily I have been led on! How " luckily " everything has gone! But if He seem to forsake me in putting me to trials of failure and things going *all* wrong, *then* will be the chance to make Him a home in my heart He will never be able to leave.

August 22nd.

. . . I have got to the middle of chapter xxii of Luke. How very vigorous is Christ's conduct—the word is too weak—how He overpowers His arresting party and His judges with a word, the bullies, during the long wait for the High Priest to get up in the morning, by His silence, and poor Peter by a look! I like the thought of Cardinal Mercier saying the Psalms for the 15th.

The thought of all the Christians great and small who read and have read the Psalms is a good thought to me. Mr. Prothero gave it of course. He mainly left me with the idea of lonely cells and glorious abbey churches, the prison, the scaffold, camps and ships' cabins, quiet homes and desert places, all sounding with those astonishing words of praise and power.

I must tell you we jog along very happily here in lovely weather. There are excursions and alarms, Majors and Colonels sweat and swear, while subaltern officers say " all bloody wind " and are justified. My section looks like being a *jolly* good one. . . . Now for a tour d'inspection, so good-bye. How good the sunshine is !

To E. P.

August 22nd.

Does this not show just what it all means,. and how trials and sorrows do but open for us access to fuller sharing in the Divine character and power ? " Not as the world giveth give I unto you," has been much in my thoughts lately. And not less so that God does give, in good measure, to them that ask Him.

Alas ! I never have a whiff of living France, except, occasionally, one can imagine that a far-distant rumble to the southward is the voice of the incomparable seventy-fives. *Vivent les soixante-quinzes !*—a thrilling cry to me.

As I wrote the date on the top of this letter, sitting by a white roadside on a hot morning of violet horizons,. my mind jumped to the story of forty-seven Augusts ago. . . . What a neighbour for the leaders of our civilisation ! What a brutal abomination ! Twice in half a century to vent a childish spite on these tenderly loved fields and villages. It is an inconceivable outrage, and raises at times in me an Old Testament cry, " Down with it, down with it—even to the ground." Samuel, Elijah, Elisha, all pronounce their culminating anathema on the rulers who made terms with their enemies. Something of their strength of soul might well be ours, but the time is not yet. First we have manfully to wipe out the stain of our own

84

meanness and poverty of outlook; but I hope the time may come when, with an authority sanctioned beyond cavil by our steadfastness and sufferings, we may be able to say to a foe beneath our heel, " We take the full responsibility for this long continuance of war. Thus would we have it, and so we will do again to you and all the sort of you."

I hate this arguing about who began the war. We should be proud to say we are fighting with all our might against the lowest conceptions of national life.

The village is infinitely touching here. It was a substantial, *soigné* little place. Out of the heaps of ruins little traces of decoration on window and pillar convey a sense of former dignity.

The largest heap was meaningless to me for days, till I noticed a single minute cross on a block of white stone. I hear that a few people have been seen coming back to look at the town of Charles Téméraire's Castle, and, gazing helplessly at the ruins, have gone pitifully away again. What an undertaking to repatriate the whole country, to win it back again from wilderness ! That will be yet another French epic.

August 23rd.

We have been having a windy time lately—but nothing more. Last night we joined the gunners in three concentrations. My four guns fired splendidly. It was great fun. The " draughtiness " brought into our line some other M.G. fellows of a very efficient, scientific company. I picked up a good deal from them, and now that my section is made up complete under my hand, I propose to get a move on, and am full of satisfaction at the prospect. With organisation gone to the wind there is never any life in anything. It is something to have got my corner into better shape. . . .

ALGERNON HYDE VILLIERS

August 24th.

I am so glad you approve of the appearance of my letters. The light by which they are written is no other than the dip or tolley.

Last night I carried out firing on my own lines, which I greatly enjoyed. When I went to explain my little arrangements to the local infantry O.C., he was highly delighted, and dewdrops were conveyed to me by the little Welshman who visited Battalion Headquarters later, and came on to me. This afternoon I have been visiting local O.P.s, and besides collecting much information to my purposes, enjoyed making acquaintance with a jolly red-headed gunner.

There were wonderful skies last night during the long hours of intermittent firing. . . .

Great wreaths of black circled the middle sky, with the starry night blue, above and below.

August 25th.

There is something very sublime about the French devotion to the soil. . . . But I should have thought their cleverness and intense acquisitive instincts were less Christian than the cheerful good-nature of the English—silly though that may often be.

Yes, the apostles and their places in the Kingdom are very pathetic, and we need to remember in our own case how silly personal ambition appears in the face of God's revelation of Himself. . . . Though Christ was not stern, yet it is clear that that sort of thing does separate us from Him, and that is what I understand by sin. . . .

Poor Esmond, or rather poor everybody else who knew him. I find I mind his loss more than I should have expected. . . . I souvenired—pinched—a table from a house in the village yesterday, and have put it at the end of the shelter, so that I can write and do

86

my calculations very comfortably now. The ugliness here is a thing to be combated.

Sunday to-morrow. I miss the weekly break, and the service which lately has grown to be so much to me. No padre ever appears except to smoke a cigarette and say "Cheeri-o"—and that only twice since I have been here—*incredibly futile*. However, my work and its success make me very happy, and I am really enjoying life thoroughly.

August 26th.

I miss my day of rest a good deal. It is the break which one values as well as the day of worship. However, I have observed it to-day by going round to my gun-positions, and, after explaining my reasons, reading them the collect, epistle, and gospel. I hope they will care to keep Sunday regularly in this way. It was a great piece of good fortune that when I had already resolved to do this, I read in a *Challenge* an excellent sermon by one Burroughs, strongly confirming my resolve.

August 27th.

Yes, it is sad to think of how Russia rose to such heights, and so sadly failed to cling to her inspiration. It must indeed be a melancholy outlook for the Czar and his family. But Russians are at their best in melancholy situations, and perhaps they will be happier at Tobolsk than they have been in Petrograd. . . .

"Yet not I, but the grace of God which is given me." St. Paul's constant confession. That is how one would have it, wouldn't one, for so only one can feel that one is building on the rock. You must not think of me as constantly *exalté*. In writing to you I often let my pen run on to say all that seems to be implied in what I hope and believe, but the splendid things of the spirit can only grow on a foundation of plain sense and quiet conviction. The confused conditions of my days, and the lack of privacy, seem to make it harder for me to catch glimpses of the Divine, but the solid belief in all that religion involves grows stronger by the struggle to keep itself in the front of one's thoughts under difficult circumstances. I expect when a more peaceful normal routine returns, I shall find I have been carried further than would now appear. Next to seeing you again, I would most like to have an hour alone in some quiet empty church, and collect all the impressions and improvisations of these recent days, review them all before God, and hear His voice to guide me. Perhaps I will have a chance to-night to do something of the sort. One company is going out and another coming in, and in this heavy rain there may well be a big gap. I am feeling rather muddly and hand-to-mouthish.

To E. P.

August 27th, 1917.

I was quite delighted by the post-cards. It was a brilliant idea of yours, and it gives me the keenest pleasure to look at them. The ugliness of my surroundings is an influence to be combated, and the lovely details of those Italian pictures give one just the sense which is most to seek out here. My favourite is the " di St. Bernardino," closely rivalled by the " dell' Oratorio." How exquisite is the front of St. Vulfran d'Abbeville! I must try to see that, but I dare say it is all protected by sandbags now. Finally, the Donatello is a crowning joy. That indeed is an inspiration of loveliness. It is really in another world than that of the Bonfiglios, isn't it ? and not to be compared to them to their detraction—but it is a higher world both in idea and execution. There is the real universal quality.

. . . . .

It is a struggle here with the crowded quarters, hours all upside-down, and generally cramped and awkward conditions, to give full play to the best things within one; but I welcome the effort and seem to see that less clear progress here may carry one farther than one would be able to go under more normal circumstances.

August 28th.

I got my little quiet spell last night, and feel much the better for it, and for a good night. The soak has been followed by a bright day, and a roaring gale, which is drying everything up in most cheering fashion.

August 29th.

I had a lovely bunch of letters last night to keep me going through a long vigil. It was a " windy " night, but nothing happened, so I was robbed of sleep, and also of the opportunity of doing something for my pets, for nothing. . . .

I have good news of myself. I shan't have to live in that foul dug-out again. Isn't that a comfort? How favoured I am in all these ways! The subsection officer is a very good fellow. He goes to church, and loves the Prayer-book. . . . There is evidence all round of an increase of scientific method in our branch of the service, which I keenly welcome. . . .

The weather is grey and stormy, but not deluging, so we are doing well.

How wonderful is the opening of St. John! There is an intense penetration in every word, which seems to reveal a whole new world. That is the mystic world, I suppose. I like to read quite short passages at a time, and let their effect sink into me.

By degrees, and especially lately, I am growing in what Smuts calls, in the speech which I so much admired, "strength of soul." An episode of to-day proves this, I think. The C.O. observed, "I hear you are holding Church services with your men," and proceeded quite kindly to make it plain that he did not wish me to proceed with the start made last Sunday. There are some R.C.s in the section, and though I remembered to make it plain that I did not want anybody to stay while I read who objected, and especially mentioned R.C.s, it seems some of them told an R.C. subaltern that they were being made to attend C. of E. services. There can be no doubt that I gave them all warning, for one, the corporal whose stripes I saved him the other day, got up, said he was an R.C., and went away. However, what with the complaint and the R.C. officer thinking it all a great joke, the C.O. *very* kindly gave me to understand that he did not wish the thing to continue. I have been able to accept this without any bitterness, and also not to mind a bit the thought of having been laughed at. That is what I mean by growth in strength of soul. As I have thought of the matter during the day, it has been almost a source of happiness, though I did not like telling the men, some of whom, I am sure, were disappointed.

Then again in the venture with the artillery, I have needed, and found, better resources than I used to have available. You see, I am doing it quite on my own, H.Q. giving a very tepid support, and being very ready to squash if anything I wanted, or did, could be objected to, and to disown altogether if anything went wrong or simply didn't come off. But I am persevering steadily and warily, and hope and believe all will turn out well. I'm sure it is the right policy. About the reading with the men the thought occurs to me : By a quite unforeseen turn of affairs, God's colours have been nailed to my mast among my brother-officers. Now, is it tempting Him to wonder whether in any sense He will let my ship go down? Will the result be that they will have occasion to blaspheme, and say, "These religious fellows are no good"? I must remember my own rule of looking in the right direction, and of Whom it was said, "He saved others, Himself He cannot save," but may I perhaps even so have, as it were, a claim for strength of soul whatever befall?

September 1st.

Yesterday morning we had a little battle. It was only a very small affair, but still, there it was—my first experience of having my guns called into action. The Boche made a raid. It was a failure, I rejoice to say, and luckily I was actually at the right spot when our fire was called for. Again *most* happily he did not shell my positions. So it was just a nice sort of trial of how we contribute to the general defence. Of course I loved it, and on the whole my fellows did quite well. Interesting points to me were brought out, and it was great fun to have everybody working, to appreciate my own part, and also the function assigned to us as a whole. The incident has bucked my men up very satisfactorily.

Then you will be glad to hear that the C.O. continues to get ahead with the work in conjunction with the artillery. I am very keen on this, as you know, and from his change of tone from assent to stimulation I surmise that the local war lords have been bringing forward the same principle, and it is well I should have been in good time with my moves in that direction.

The weather is very stormy, but the rain is reasonably moderate, for which one cannot be too thankful. Last night was exquisite. The moon blazed from 8 p.m. to 5 in the morning out of an almost cloud-

less sky. One could see all the distances in hazy
silhouette, and at dawn she went down bright orange
into a bank of dark powder-blue cloud. I do enjoy
the skies here. One is driven to look at them more
than one is used to by the sadness of the landscape.
The battalion from the county of my first camp is
here now, and I like being with them. The company
living in this shelter is commanded by a very clever
and agreeable Jew.

September 2nd.

I have been more fearfully busy the last twenty-four
hours than I think I ever was before. At this point
I must tell you that sleep overcame me, and I am going
on now after four hours' most refreshing slumber.
This will go down by my runner at dawn. It is
wonderful how well I am learning to sleep irregularly,
and make up a good amount of rest by adding two or
three bits together. It gives one a good sense of another
point mastered. . . .

You will be pleased I know, that my stunt with the
artillery came off yesterday evening, and was a brilliant
success—quite beyond anything I had expected.
Accuracy was really remarkable. Fun to make a
sentry bob quickly down at 2,000 yards using indirect
fire—*i.e.* not being able to see him at the firing-point.
The whole thing directed and observed by me perched
in an eerie litle loft in the roof of a ruin—telephone,
telescope, all complete. Report to G.O.C.—D.S.O.
or at least M.C. confidently expected !! But seriously,
it is proud for me to feel that I have transformed my
little corner of the M.G. world. Not with special
references to myself, an infantry Tom thanked me
yesterday for the work of the company the other
morning. " It did us good," he said. . . .

I would not oppose Martha and Mary at bottom.
There cannot be two right ways of approaching life

between which we are obliged to make a compromise. One must fix on Jesus Himself, Who was perfectly spiritual and perfectly practical, and each because He was the other. He might have been a voice crying in the wilderness, or a constructive statesman, but he failed in neither direction, because the two tendencies were in Him perfectly balanced. I would take the position myself that the seeking first of the Kingdom of God is the true common sense, and similarly that in the common, straightforward course of life the deep things of God are unveiled.

Yes, indeed I agree that we must ask God's help against the powers of darkness. Strength of soul— that is my motive phrase just now—to be conquerors for righteousness' sake. That is the way I think we may reasonably ask for *things* of God, *i.e.* side by side and only in relation to the power to use such things for His ends. Such a prayer admits of no disappointment. It is only in another form the deepest prayer of all which cannot be uttered before it is answered—" Thy Kingdom come."

Yes, Ll. G. and Kerensky have a certain quality which by its rarity in public men wears a heaven-sent air, but I stick to the balance, and plump for E. G. As Mr. G. wrote of Lord Aberdeen, " All the parts in which he was great are the foundation-stones of our nature. . . . Time is their witness and their friend, and in the final distribution of posthumous fame Lord A. has nothing to forfeit, he has only to receive." Fame may or may not be E. G.'s fate. It is an indifferent matter. But his patience, wisdom, and honour are established facts in the history of our nation, which may be ignored, but cannot be undone.

We must expect no spiritual revival while the war lasts. I see that. Men are too tired and jumpy, too much absorbed by the passionate longing to be done with the horrible job. In many ways they are smaller

93

at the moment, not greater, but in human life and character every time is seed-time and harvest at once, and as we are now reaping as we have sown, we can believe that we are also sowing to a certain happier harvest. Good-bye—day will soon be dawning. Avanti.

To E. M. R.

September 3rd, 1917.

Yes, we have had fine days. One looks at, and cares about the sky a great deal here where the earth is so pitifully sad. You need, or I do or did, to see it every day, this melancholy *abimé* landscape, in order to realise what an awful sin it is to preach war and deliberately practise it. One feels, too, that the simple avocations of men, toiling and building, gathering and spending, are more in line with a beneficent purpose in the world than one thought—that God needs man as gardener to His world, in the thought of the first Bible legend.

May we have strength of soul to withstand to the end, and mete out so awful a punishment as would have satisfied even a Psalmist. Most likely we shall fail in so supremely difficult a part. . . .

There is room for an inspired Avenger.

September 4th.

Did you read a *letter* in the —— about Humour and Humility, in which the writer said that St. John was full of humour, and instances especially Nicodemus —the whole incident ? I cannot see the humour of *it*, can you ? but with the general statement I quite agree, and I should instance first the calling of Nathanael, where every saying is smiling, so to speak. With the

94

woman of Samaria there are clear gleams too, I think, "In that saidst thou truly," *e.g.* The whole point is important, to my thinking, for the conventional teaching of the Divine Nature is far too stilted, and must be expanded to include a great deal more than it commonly does now, if it is not to prove inadequate and be forsaken when apparently conflicting "goods" come strongly before the mind. I was praying the other day to be able to hold fast to the faith of the universal sovereignty of the Divine by realising better the fullness of Him Who filleth all in all. We must learn to worship God not only as Love and Justice, Wisdom and Mercy, but also as Gaiety and Simplicity and Ardour, for one cannot afford a one-sided conception of the All Good and Great. Our thought must have no flanks which can be turned.

September 5th.

The day before yesterday I had a very tart exchange of notes with Jingle. He is building himself a spacious winter palace, and will not spare a man to help my tiny teams to make themselves a shelter. It is too bad, for they *all* always have to be up half the night on guard, and have to find for themselves entirely as to cooking, getting rations, clearing up, etc. . . . .

The thought of Christ sleeping in the storm is always wonderful magic, isn't it? One must face and appreciate His degree of detachment, and triumph over the things which agitate us. It is almost the central feature of His revelation, I think, combined as it is in Him with intense realisation of the other world, and power to reign in that sphere here on earth. I was reading chapter v this morning and verse 44 brought me up short. "How *can* ye believe that receive honour one of another, and seek not the honour that cometh from God only?" I have to

lay that to heart very closely. No man's favour, or
the expectation of his approval, must turn me in future,
and God be my only recompense. How happy one
would be then, wouldn't one? . . . I follow you
absolutely in the instinctive sense of direct contact
with Christ and his surroundings in St. John's Gospel.
He must have been there. Though the artistry is
plain all through, so too is the essential veracity and
lack of " composition." There is nothing *made up*
about it all, is there?

Yes, I noticed the interpretation of Peter's " I go
a fishing "—very sure, I think. Christ had commanded them otherwise; the first day they got back
into those boats was a day of crisis for the whole world,
and so Christ came and called them back. How kind
He is to them too, though poor Peter has to be grieved.

My corner of the shelter is rather dark for sticking
up the post-cards. I prefer to be able to have them
out on my table. But I have a pot with lovely white
phlox in it, which I found blowing in a forsaken garden,
and I have stuck up the Millet. The young man and
woman going to work in just such fields as these—they
are what one so cruelly misses, looking over these
slopes even on such a divine evening as was yesterday's.

September 6th, 1917.

Events have taken a delightful turn. The transport
officer has gone sick, and I go to take his place. I am
now at H.Q. waiting for my *horse*—think of it—to
come up for me. I have just told Harrison to get my
spurs out, which I haven't worn for a month. It
will be the most pleasant change. . . . I write this
now, in case I find on getting down there that I have
a good deal to do before I start up again with the
limbers. How I shall enjoy the relative privacy down
there! The place is actually Epehy. There is only

the padre there. I have met him—he is an R.C., but seems a very attractive fellow, and by all accounts is an educated man.

Here the horse was signalled. He turned out to be Jingle's grey mare, as rough a broken-winded old screw as you could find, but I pushed her along a good pace, and here I am, full of excellent tea, and rejoicing in the prospect of my valise and pyjamas and every manner of good thing from stables to sketching. It is said that, once taken into hospital, a man usually manages to stay there a month or so. I hardly hope for such a holiday, and in one way it would be rather too long. At present, however, it seems one could not have too much of such palatial surroundings. The hut shared by the padre and me is four or five times the size of the shelter occupied by the officers of an infantry company, four to seven and myself. It is divided into two rooms, and has windows and doors, and I shall have a wash-hand-stand, and once more pyjamas.

What luck! just when I was getting a bit stale and quarrelsome, I am afraid. However, I was bearing the critical moment of getting into the collar after the first novelty capers, with the consciousness of God's help, and with much comfort from St. John.

I had a very happy read this morning of chapter vi. I felt so much sympathy with the people who asked, What must we do that we may work the works of God ? As you and I may look at our own lives, " Why," may we not ask, " do we not see God's power more clearly manifested in us ? " We are trying to come to Christ with a real belief in Him, conviction, that is, that, as St. Peter felt, we have no other to go to, and He says that he that cometh He will in no wise cast out. Is God playing us false ? one must ask in order to be quite honest. Towards an answer I start with two obvious contributions. First, that, in any view you and I are singularly happy people, and that we may with reverence thank God for His grace that is given unto us. In spite of all our faults, we are growing in the mastery of life, and are rich in some of the best blessings. The second thought is that the life of Jesus, in which we must see the only complete answer God has been able to give to the question What shall we do? shows us that God's giving is not as the world's. We, you and I, have still far to go before we have learnt the lesson—What to ask of God, and what are those good things which God has prepared for them that love Him. So in the end we seem to reach the conclusion Christ Himself so often declared. *Only* believe. We do not know even what our true good is. We are so utterly dependent *in fact* upon God that there is no other way open to the spirit of man than to follow suit to the lead of plain palpable circumstances and believe—

> "All that thou sendest me
>   In mercy given,
> Angels to beckon me
> Nearer, my God, to Thee,
>   Nearer to Thee."

Those are truly great words, I think, and the thought places one at the very centre of the true religious experience. It is the voice of Charles seeking you in his troubles, and in the act of perfect seeking (perfect because untrammelled by a shade of doubt or self-consciousness) actually finding what he needs. Just to be nearer to God —that is the aim of life, the function proper to human nature. The wish, hope, aim, or whatever we call it, seems to be ours, the power to get there, to get to Him, seems to be His entirely. So every time our waking thoughts, waking from our sleep of misguided selfishness, will be bright with His praise.

The flies have invaded this hut in thousands, and I play the Abdou game on them in vain. However, they are not the equals of their oriental brothers, thank goodness, in their powers of vexation—an easy-going race of insects compared with their pestiferous fellows of the desert. . . .

When I had finished my letter to you last night, I went out and inspected the parade of limbers " proceeding up the line." Bits *filthy*, my dear! You wouldn't believe such a state of things. So I kicked up the necessary how-de-do and expect a great change before long. Then I came in and dined, and at dusk mounted a stout bay, and pushed off in pursuit of the transport. You may imagine I was not long at H.Q., with a vision of certain pink things reposing on a white pillow at the head of a soft jaeger bag calling to me across the night! Swiftly we trotted home, and I gave myself up to the luxury of sleep in civilised conditions—surely there is no greater blessing than a good bed. I read the Psalms first though, especially my favourite xxxiv. Verses 5, 8, 10, and 11 are exquisite. The day before, No. xxvii, one of the very greatest, was good to meet again. This morning I was able to have a real good leisurely " read " in perfect peace, which I enjoyed beyond everything. The first eleven verses of Psalm xxxvii are very beautiful, and I like to think of the whole as the " Rabbi Ben Ezra " of the Book (v. 25). Later I read St. John vii and viii. One sees far more clearly than elsewhere all the stupid hostility that Christ was up against. How discouraging it must have been, and how amazing is His dauntless self-assertion—dedication!—is it not both fully, seeing the circumstances ? His half-reluctance to go up to the Feast, and the Jews' manifestly deadly antipathy ? Yet, what triumphs Christ draws from under His enemies' very noses! The officers who dare not touch Him, the accusers of the woman His purity so terribly confounds, His perfect confidence that physically God has determined the hour of His final offering of His body, so that no plottings or conspiracies of violence can reach Him before the moment which God's purpose requires. It is all a marvellous revelation. It is God Himself indeed Who stands revealed.

I have looked at my X. sketch and I think it can become something possibly. This afternoon, however, must be devoted to a bath! Luxe upon luxe! Think of me *very* full of beans.

September 8th.

Last night I got the transport officer's message that he was coming out of hospital to-day. What's more, he has actually come—tactless fellow. However, though I must go back to the line to-night, I feel ever so much refreshed by my outing. I am going to try and squeeze in a sketch before going up to-night. It is very hard for a padre to be anything but a cheerio visitor, one sees that; but it is none the less a lack in our social life that there are no " holy men " going about. They would have their drawbacks too, no doubt. I read the man born blind this morning, just right! It is indeed splendid. What must have been the feelings of the woman of Samaria and the blind man when the supreme revelation was made point blank at them. How significant it seems that they should have been, too, quite stray people. But of course nobody was stray to Christ. I much agree with you about the authorship, and specially do I respond to your words " that never-to-be-forgotten Feast." What a memory it was to him. " In the last day, that great day of the feast, Jesus stood and cried, saying, If any man thirst——" How do you think it all happened ? I expect men were crowding round Him as He sat and trying to hear Him talking, and He would suddenly get up, and in His unique way of blended passion and calm carry them away into a world of new ideas and expanded horizons.

Now I must pack away those too much but too briefly enjoyed pink garments, and then try a sketch.

September 9th.

You can't think how much the better I feel for my two nights at the transport. I am taking up my jobs here with a sense of freshness which is very satisfactory after so short a rest. That first month was rather hard work, I expect, being the *first*, with all the novelty to engage one's mind and use up one's powers. I enjoyed it, of course, but I am conscious that it was a strain. Now I feel very calm and collected, with things well in hand so to speak.

It was the most admirable plan my doing that sketch. I enjoyed it at the moment, and I think it is very successful, but the fact of having done it—the recollection of doing it—is most delightful and has given me pleasure ever since. It took me out of war interests so completely for the moment, although it was inevitably a war subject—just a ruin and a hut against the evening sky. I think you will like it. I had a good clean up while I was away, clothes and body and boots have all come back revived. I wore my slacks, and my nice tunic, and my leggings and my slippers, all the things I cannot have here, with a childish joy, but the best was the cap, I think. The steel hat is not a convenient head-gear.

The animals, too, were a great joy. The majority were mules. It was an interesting thing to be in close touch with them. I thought them such ugly, pathetic creatures, looking conscious of their irregular breeding. The meanest horse has more carriage, and any donkey a more satisfied air. The crossed animal looks it all over. But they are very good and quiet and healthy, and good workers, and one feels it very hard that they should seem to be a little ashamed of themselves.

It was a delightful interlude, and I shall linger over it for many days, I hope. We are having a wonderful spell of weather, aren't we ? The mists in the morning are the only drawback, as we have to stand-to till they lift. The complete absence of northern news is exciting. I suppose we shall wait till it rains again ! Was there anything so lamentable as the Russians. Where will it end ?

September 10th.

I like the article . . . on the need for more thought. That thoughtlessness and a disregard for the value of truth are among our chief vices, is very true, I think. Most people do take *everything* at second hand, and without reflection, don't they ? I occasionally have time for a dip into d'Artagnan. I do like it so much. There is something so fresh and overflowing about him—a delightful creation, and most refreshing to come in contact with.

It is something of that sort which may for a moment threaten the pale Nazarene. But after a moment's thought one sees how one is only the victim of a silly convention about Jesus in having such a thought. On the contrary, the threat is soon turned into an illumination of the spontaneity, daring, and unconquerable mind of the great adventurer. . . . I suppose such language is irreverent, but one must be irreverent to be real, don't you think ? Any other way of thinking of Christ our Saviour allows to rival ideals a tacit existence beside His own, and involves a betrayal of Him by the failure honestly to use the simple straightforward revelation of Himself which He has given us.

September 12th.

It is a new experience for me to be writing to you at 9.30 in the morning. It has been very foggy, which necessitates a long watch, and also gave an opportunity for getting on with some work which cannot be done in bright light for fear of observation, but which had been getting all behind, and required my personal supervision. It is nice to have a perfectly quiet moment; all the others are still asleep. It is amusing to find the Brigadier taking up his pen, and recommending the very course which I have got going in this corner. The fact was very cordially recognised at Battalion H.Q.

To E. P.

September 13th.

The Italian P.C.s are again deeply interesting. Anything of the kind is acutely delightful to me just now. I can't tell you how much I am enjoying *Les Trois Mousquetaires*. It is inimitable. The pure air of romance one breathes in its pages is refreshing in the extreme.

Renan's paper—*Qu'est ce qu'une Nation?*—I have also intensely enjoyed. That is the sort of thing which can only be done in French prose. It reminds me of Guizot, but is more brilliant in point of style. It is touching, at this moment, to see how experience cannot be kept out of sight, in spite of the most solemn resolutions of detachment and impartiality. . . .

The account of the building of the wall of Nehemiah is strikingly appropriate to this modern warfare; " one far from another" is only too often true of our posts.

The conduct of the R.C.s was positively comic in its microcosmic conforming to a tradition which its age and consistency almost make a great one. " No quarter" has ever been their cry, but it is really amusing to see the same spirit coming out so promptly on such a tiny occasion. No other opportunity is likely to turn up, I am afraid.

September 13th.

I had to go some way back to get to the dentist, and enjoyed seeing fresh country from an R.A.M.C. motor. In the morning, too, coming down from H.Q. on my horse, I made a detour and had a lovely gallop. " My joy no man taketh from you " is a glorious thought. . . .

The T.O. tells me that Jingle admits that the war has been his chance, and says he thinks J. never had any position or decent income in his life before. To my mind this accounts for a great deal, and explains, if it does not excuse, his wretched attitude towards those above him.

September 14th.

I had a jolly ride up the now familiar ways from the transport to H.Q. I have been much occupied making two beautiful little charts for this combination stunt of the Brigadier's. They produced many approving comments from my friends at Battalion H.Q. We made a first trial this evening, and everything worked well, except for the lack of light, which we could not help, and for certain defects in the position which Jingle insisted upon my taking up. He is one of those difficult people to whom Macaulay's amusing sentences about James II and listening to reason conspicuously apply.

However, I have quite made up my mind to take everything very calmly and make the best of things as they come, rather than dwell on thoughts of how much better I should manage things !

We have had a few showers to-day. The roads are truly deplorable. The least thing covers them with a slime which hugs one's boots, and makes walking a perfect nuisance. The flying boys have the best of it *after* the transport people. The former were doing great feats to-night. It was great to see them against a very fierce sky—one sees the black puffs of smoke soiling the sky around them, and then well after comes the bang, by which time the pilot has swerved or mounted, and is sailing away again in the most nonchalant fashion. I have never seen one brought down yet—by either side. . . .

September 15th.

As the days go by, and no decisive military action is taken, one is more and more inclined to think that the next move will be some sort of ultimatum from the Yanks. Whether the Huns will cave in to Wilson or not remains to be seen. I should not myself be too certain of it. The American terms will be sufficiently drastic, one supposes, or the Huns would close with them, and keep their Kaiser, which would be no good. If the terms are as they should be, the Kaiser's Government would have no ground for accepting them and committing suicide, and the question remains whether there is any other body of opinion in Germany capable of speaking for the nation, and giving Wilhelm the go-by. . . .

What you say of the influence of such books as Mr. Glover's is very true. I quite think that a more emancipated frame of mind in approaching the Gospels and religion in general is one of the only hopes remaining to us. At present, as J—— said to me at Camiers, a man who reads the Bible is *prima facie* set down as a fool—at any rate by men of his generation, and I expect that is because such people have equipped themselves with a second-hand idea of what they would find in the Bible if they studied it at all. To approach any religious thought or act in this way involves repudiating the whole thing, so it seems to me, and it was the thing Christ always inveighed against, wasn't it ?   He is the great champion of mental freedom, I think.

You put that matter of praise of men and the service of God exactly right.   The relative indifference thus formed proceeds from the concentration on the latter. But there is clearly a danger of revising the relation between the two.   Would you not say that vanity and personal ambition—the last infirmity—are among the most successful opponents of the spirit of Truth ?

The Dean on the Logos doctrine is truly splendid reading, and uplifts me by its noble width of confidence.   I like the emphasis on knowledge.   That which we study to know passes inevitably into what we are actually becoming.   One does feel that the mass of men are totally ignorant about God—have no ideas about Him whatever.   In this way one is inclined to say that conventional religious teaching and practice do more harm than good.

September 16th.

. . . The General has come down heavily in favour of the co-operation methods I claim to have introduced.   Consequently I have had a long morning lying out in the sun, occasionally having a shoot, and shall soon go back for evening straffing.   *The* critical issue remains in the balance, however.   Will he, or will he not, let one gun for this duty off night duty ? Otherwise we are undone.

September 17th.

Life among the silences of the hills is indeed a soothing, happy thought, and I do believe we should be able to make that sort of life what it appears to be to the distant imagination. . . . But whether in the hills, or the plains, growth in the power of the spirit will be slow but sure.   It will indeed be a rich harvest for the short time of earthly life, if at its close we can feel that we have so grown into the knowledge and love of God that we understand how He works, and how we can be fellow-workers with Him. Perhaps, too, we may hope to hand on to our children some idea of the possibility and supreme value of such an attainment. I was reading last night the mighty fourteenth chapter of St. John, " Let not your heart be troubled." We may, I think, take that blessed work to ourselves, for according to our lights we do indeed believe in God, and also in Christ. By " believing " I mean that we cannot now contemplate a life in which the revelation of Jesus Christ is not the most precious possession. Our achievement may be small, our progress a mere groping, but let us repeat Pascal's " Thou wouldst not seek me if thou hadst not found me." I must leave you for to-day, with thoughts which carry us above all the changes and chances into the world of peace and stillness where God reigns and welcomes us.

To Charles Villiers (aged 5)

September 17th, 1917.

I was ever so pleased to get your letter last night, and as for the blackberry jelly, it is the most delicious thing I ever did taste.

I am glad to hear you are having such a jolly time. But you must never make a " row " before 7 o'clock or at any other time.

Germans make rows. You should have heard them last night. I must admit we began it, but they started banging about all over the shop, and sending up rockets like a firework show. You shall have fireworks for your birthday when you are six, and then you will know what the Germans do when we frighten them. Up in the air go red lights and green lights, and great blazing stars which make everything as plain as day-light for a mile round. Then they have a splendid golden rain which comes down in a gleaming fountain. It is altogether a pretty sight, but usually there is such a racket going on at the same time that one cannot enjoy it thoroughly—field guns going "Whiiiiiiiiiz-bang," and trench mortars going "Crrrump, crrrump," and machine guns barking like a pack of dogs.

September 18th.

We had a great success to-day. A party of Boche workers was reported from the O.P., and pouff went down five out of ten, and the rest scuttled for a trench, so the observer declares. This shows that the lay-out of the lines by me is accurate to a T. I am awfully pleased about it.

September 19th.

Yesterday's letter came at the close of a happy day —the good shooting, and in the evening the finding of some splendid Michaelmas daisies, yellow daisies and beautiful scarlet-leaved stuff, in a wilderness garden, which I brought home to adorn the " dining-room," in an elegant shell-case for a flower-pot. It was a wonderful sunset evening, and there was a calm glow which made even this country look happy. . . .

September 20th.

I read the Litany this morning after the joyful Psalms. It is wonderfully beautiful, the picture of the perfectly ordered private and public life is a triumph, but alas ! how well the " miserable sinners " is justified by the contrast of that picture and this. . . .
All goes well here. The date of our relief seems to hold good. I shall be very glad of it, and especially for the men, who are getting pretty well fagged. They will have been three solid months in the trenches,

LETTERS FROM FRANCE

I remember one or two excellent leaders and notes
in the *Challenge* which seemed to bring Christ's mind
to bear on our common lives. That is what one wants,
to my mind, and what the clergy cannot manage to
do for us in nine cases out of ten. They seem to live
in a world of their own, don't they ? and clerical shop
is as remote from most men's concerns as clergymen's
clothes are unthinkable for some people's costume.
I remember a sermon at Belton—the last I have heard,
by the way—in which the preacher begged his hearers
not to be ashamed of being Christians and standing
up for Christ in their billets. That would have been
all very well if the men he had been talking to had
been in any real sense professing Christians or conscious
of any obligation or loyalty towards Christ. But
I'm perfectly sure that the vast majority of them
needed to be made Christians first before it was
conceivable that they should be ashamed of professing
Christ. Nor had they in all probability any idea of
what they were being asked to stand up for, beyond a
sort of conventional piety and righteousness. Airing
that sort of thing they would immediately know to
be impossibly priggish conduct for them, or indeed
for anybody. My contention is that we don't half
know, and are not being taught, what Christianity
was, or is, or ever shall be.

It is very interesting to hear of your reading the great
Durham Bishop on St. John. Temple quotes him in
Mens Creatrix as saying that St. John, Origen, and
Browning had been the master influences on his mind.
Pollock had a favourite story of him. Some one was
arguing that all sport fostered a combative or com-
petitive instinct, and the Bishop asked whether that
could be said of battledore and shuttle-cock ! The
speech is no doubt disproportionate, like the Duke of
W.'s oath, to the greatness of its author. I wish

we had a towering figure among the Bishops. A great ecclesiastic is a good thought, but no doubt with cathedrals they are out of date! . . .

September 23rd.

There was a magnificent " straf " by us (within sight of this) last night. It really was a glorious sight, and its effect must have been deuced unpleasant for the Boche.

I have had another interesting day in my O.P., and am making great progress in the very difficult job of map-spotting—*i.e.* finding the exact position on the map of an object seen through the telescope. We have had some quite successful shoots, and our reports figure prominently in Brigade Intelligence Summaries.

September 24th.

" Come, Wm., let us sing the ninetieth Psalm," [1] is capital.

The 18th day is a great day. Side by side with the humble and contrite ones there are at least as many rejoicing in the power of the Lord to sustain victoriously, aren't there ?

I saw a magnificent sight to-day—a fleet of some twenty of our planes going over. The sun was low. behind them, and they looked all golden as they swarmed above us. I don't know what they were after.

September 26th.

. . . Yesterday was *the* day for which we have been working up for the past week. . . .

It was a great affair. The heavies were up and were firing all day, and at dusk the fun began. By

[1] Luther speaking to Melanchthon.

Jove! it was magnificent. The great feature was the burning oil, which bursts in great sheets of flame, lighting up the whole scene with a savage brilliance. M.G.s were in great force, and the heavies poured forth their huge crumps in an endless strain. Sudden momentary silences occur, which is odd. You think something has happened, the stillness is so deep, and in a second or two the chorus opens again. The Boche line was a chaos of smoke and flame. At first one felt the bombardment a glorious spectacle, but as it went grinding on through the hour and ten minutes of its hideous course I began to feel it was horrible and hideous only. There was something dreary about the one-sidedness of it. The Boche put back a certain amount of stuff, but broadly one had the sense of our just grinding him down laboriously, unimaginatively, almost ridiculously. Altogether it is a Boche business, to my mind, a bombardment. We should never have done that sort of thing if he had not taught us.

I can feel no pity for him. He has brought us down to his beastly level in too many ways.

The infantry had a pretty hot time, and had about as many casualties as the number of my old home in Sloane Street. My nice little friend the Captain has been killed, I am sorry to say. But the damage done is reckoned to have been very heavy, and the whole raid to have been a thorough success.

From daylight to 9 o'clock I was strafing the place where the Boche was probably trying to get things right under cover of the mist, and did not get to bed till ten. So I have been sleeping serenely all day, and enjoyed it enormously.

September 28th.

Ever since the show I have been as busy as a bee —really not more than time to eat and sleep—the latter a minimum. It is obvious that after the tremendous hammering of the other day, a lot of work has got to be put in by Brer Boche, if he is to get his house in order again.

Consequently we have been strafing him day and night at short intervals ever since. . . .

We had a casualty last night while firing. This time it was M.G.s which got on to us. The man was of course a particularly good one. His wound is not dangerous, I'm glad to say.

I am with the gun now in a cosy corner of trench, safely removed from the spot where the shells came and sitting in a pleasant sunshine. From time to time we send over a message of heartfelt hate to likely spots across the way. It would be quite harmless if I could get proper relief, but dawn to dusk is rather a long time, and I don't like to leave the sergeant, except for quite a short space. On top of this the night-firing is rather a burden. However, I got four hours' sleep last night, but none the night before, and only a short spell during yesterday.

September 29th.

. . . The comparison of the "Benedic, anima mea" (Psalm civ) to a great picture is true indeed, and there can hardly be a greater, more universal poem than the great song of praise. It is good to remember that our lives are set in the midst of so many and great glories, and that the glorious majesty of the Lord shall endure for ever, the Lord shall rejoice in His works. The two Psalms (civ and cvii) taken together seem to be a genuinely adequate treatment of the illimitable thought of God, the splendour of His expression in nature, and the unfailing "stability" of His dealing with man. For He satisfieth the empty soul, and filleth the hungry soul with goodness. . . .

There is a danger of the *Challenge* degenerating into

á specialist paper, always uninteresting *à la longue*, and where religion is concerned just another feature of the whole attitude needing to be reversed. I like what you say of the need for natural handling of great subjects. A stilted attitude is so much worse than blank ignorance or indifference.

I often think how strange it is to be surrounded by young men of many excellences, good-humoured, kindly, not unduly coarse many of them, and with plenty of courage and capacity, but, as far as one knows, living quite without thought of God. However, for a long time I was ostensibly the same, though a seed must have been growing all the time. My quotation from Pascal has a nice origin. I found it in a little book which I bought in glorious St. Botolph's at Boston under the stump. . . .

This letter has been constantly interrupted by cheerful visitors, and by aeroplanes from time to time. We have to keep a look-out for them.

September 30th.

We have had some fun shooting to-day. Aeros have been in great force on both sides, and we have had one or two other good targets. . . .

All the writing I have seen, or seen commented on, in the matter of God and omnipotence is vitiated, to my mind, by the ignoring of the essential fact, so firmly grasped by the two greatest Christians of all time, St. Paul and St. John, that God is not only above us, but in us. To set Him over against His world, and say what can He, or can He not, do with it, is a hopeless way of approaching the question. Some form of Logos idea is vital.

The relieving man turned up while I was writing this. I sent him away for a moment, but he now returns.

ALGERNON HYDE VILLIERS

It has been most refreshing to escape to this comparatively peaceful spot, almost out of hearing of the guns, and quite free of the long-spun-out feeling of responsibility. Two letters this morning completed the joy of the sunshine and the freedom of the hour.

My friends of the nicest battalion (Suffolks) have been at the neighbouring Battalion H.Q. lately, and I have enjoyed being *au mieux* with them. They are, of course, the heroes of last week's show, and very pleased with the way their gallant men conducted themselves.

That brings me to R.'s article. I thought it quite in his worst manner—overdone for a start, and merely provocative. If he had been able to tell us in what way the fighting-men propose to reconstruct there would have been some point in the article. I am pretty sure they have no ideas on the subject, nor are they likely to have them in future simply as fighting-men. No one could reverence the incomparable "foot" more than I, but I feel it quite absurd that their greatness should be made the ground of a padre's sneers at people who are ventilating more hopeful ideas in a better spirit than was formerly the case, by reason of the very work which they are doing so splendidly.

HAVRE,
October 3rd.

It seems such a simple thing just to cross the Channel after the amazing effort of getting thus far. I must tell you all about it. I started on the night of my last letter—Monday—and rode down by lovely moonlight to the terminus of the light railway. We bumbled along by the roadside, and got to X.[1] at about 1.30 in the morning. I had rather a nice companion—

[1] Péronne.

an artillery officer. I always rather like them. The R.T.O. at X. announced that the Havre train was off, and all officers going on leave were now proceeding via Boulogne. There was a supply train which might or might not reach Havre by 1 a.m. the following morning. Very little encouraged by this news, I went to the club, and found every bed occupied. So I nodded uneasily in a chair, and dropped off to sleep perhaps about 5, waking just in time to get breakfast and catch the Amiens train. I had made up my mind to go that far by the Boulogne train, and see what could be done from there. It was a lovely morning, and the marshy Somme was as picturesque as ever. I saw quite a lot of moorhens. A genial French *commerçant* got in, and sat next to me, and we had a long conversation on the war. He was very warlike, and very admiring of Sir D. H. and of our armies. We exchanged many compliments, and I found his loathing of the Boche very sympathetic. He was from near Metz, so, as he said, he knew all about them ; my reading of Dumas has quite revived my French, and I enjoyed talking.

When I got to Amiens, there seemed to be no hope of getting here except by Paris, which would have been as long a business as the supply train. So I thought I must go by it, and was consulting with a jovial *facteur* on the supply train platform as to when it was likely to arrive, when a French supply train rolled in which was going as far as Rouen. I implored it to wait five minutes, hurriedly wired to Father to send his car to meet me at Rouen at 4, bought some excellent pears, sandwiches, and choc., and jumped into the funny little guard's compartment, and off we went. The country was looking radiant. It is very hilly, and thickly clothed with trees. All the smiling happiness of the farm-workers and orchards was a joy to behold. The normal functioning of life

is beautiful. The common getting and spending and
caring for the kindly fruits is surely part of God's plan.
At Rouen Station there was no motor, so I telephoned
here, and found that Father had set off in it to meet
me. We chased each other from one station to
another—there are five in Rouen—but met at last.

The motor tore up the steepest precipices along the
noble Seine valley through Caudebec and to jolly old
Havre in time for dinner.

2 PLACE FREDERIC SAUVAGE, HAVRE,
October 4th, 1917.

I have just returned from a most successful expedition with Monsieur le Ministre to Caudebec and
Jumièges. The former is a dear little village on the
edge of the river, with the quaintest old streets, a fine
flamboyant Gothic church—a mass of bewildering lace-
like decoration—and a beautiful airy frontage on the
water. It was a grey, clear morning, the river looking
steely, and the trees very dark against the sky. There
were many regrets for the sunshine, but I quite enjoyed
the neutral tint of the thoroughly French scene. The
country we passed through is really beautiful, and
with a character quite its own. The ground is very
steep and broken, and the woods and fields jumbled
up together with an attractive air of prosperous
profusion. Little roads wind about the valleys, and
big roads zigzag up the high *côtes*. Luncheon was
delicious, needless to say—omelettes and Camembert.
We went on to Jumièges, a superb ruin. All that
remains is *de l'onzième*, though there were additions
du quatorzième, since demolished. The simplicity of
the entrance and the soaring height of the chancel
arch leave memorable impressions.

The garden steps are of original and engaging plan.

Unfortunately, the weather seems to have broken,
but nothing can seriously detract from my enjoyment

of my clean sheets and frequent baths, and of the joyful sense of relaxation from the responsibilities of command! How pompous!

I enjoyed meeting my beloved twentieth Psalm this morning. The fourth of the month is another good day with nineteenth and twentieth in the morning, and matchless twenty-third in the evening. M. Hymans, a distinguished, very clever Belgian, told us at luncheon that M. P. Cambon had said of Mr. Asquith, " C'est l'homme d'état qui a connu quand il fallait faire la guerre, et c'est l'homme d'état qui saura quand il faut faire la paix."

October 5th.

I have got such a lot of interesting things to tell you that I hope I shall make up for my scrappy letter of yesterday.

The dinner-party on Thursday was a delightful experience. . . . I had the most amusing talk with my host, M. Ancel, and with le Gouverneur du Havre, Amiral Didelot. The former has the very cleverest face and the most engaging ease and polish of manner. I liked meeting a Frenchman who one felt at once was quite first-class. He gave an inimitable *récit* of the Bolo Pasha incident. The inconvenience *les hauts personnages* involved must submit to in the matter he spoke of in a deprecating vein of amusement quite inconceivable in an Englishman under similar circumstances. It made one reflect that they must feel the core of their national life quite beyond the reach of any adverse influence from such affairs. The attitude, at any rate, conveys an admirable absence of self-consciousness.

M. Ancel, in his unflurried, analysing way, is splendid on the Boche. His estimate of their intellectual level, expressed entirely without heat, brought home to one what the threat of German domination means to France.

117

ALGERNON HYDE VILLIERS

The admiral was a charming figure, tall and spare, and full of animation. He gave the most deplorable account of parties of Russian sailors that he had had to deal with. They straggled in at any time, half of them drunk, and their officers declined to take any disciplinary measures whatever. Eventually they were persuaded to get on board a French ship. The captain of it subsequently reported that the men formed a Soviet to control things on board, and that a fresh member announced himself as president every day.

The admiral said that Edward VII. would have been a great asset to the Entente, as he would have been accepted as the titular chief of the whole alliance. One knows about French sentiment for him, but this is a new notion of the extent of their regard.

Both Ancel and Didelot were very grave about their losses, and absolutely unfaltering and unqualified in their expressions of determination to go on till the Boche was beat.

Their eulogy of our efforts was wonderfully understanding. . . .

I shall always remember the evening, for the impression one had of genuine regard and affection existing between these men and women of the two nations, and delighting to give itself expression in unmistakable looks and words.

, The next day was for Belgium, when M. Hymans came to luncheon. He is just retiring from being Minister in London. I told you of M. Cambon's saying about Mr. Asquith. Hymans gave a wonderful account of the Crown Council at the Palace in Brussels on the night of August 2nd, 1914. When they came out after half an hour's unanimity in face of the ultimatum, the principal stairs were crowded with every sort of person who could gain access to the place, asking desperately, "Nous resistons ? Nous resistons ?" and when they said, "Yes," "Ils étaient comme transformés."

He says that the sufferings of the Belgians are becoming more acute every day, and their hatred of the Boche more intense. There will be a hopeless shortage of food before long. The situation in this respect has been serious for some months. Instead of attempting to conciliate them, the Germans go on taking every opportunity to terrorise and insult them, and the spirit of the people remains undaunted. . . . The one bright spot is the appearance in Brussels every day of a small Belgian paper which the Germans would give their eyes to suppress, but the secret of its production, by a miracle, remains, to their rage, absolutely undiscoverable.

All this *grandeur d'âme* on the part of the Belgians was a revelation to me. Father assures me that it is all true. Every day the Belgian papers here have the same story, every official he meets feels the same furious loathing of the enemy. I urged Hymans to take every means in his power to make the public with us realise the situation more vividly. Nothing could be a better correction to peace-talk at home.

My visit and holiday end in a few hours. A motor has been found to take me as far as Amiens, so my return will be very much quicker than my coming here. . . .

I was greatly struck by Psalm xxxvi this morning. The picture of the foolish " ungodly," all over the place, deceiving himself and others, is very acute ; and then follows so splendidly, not a picture of the good man, but " *Thy* Mercy, O Lord, *Thy* faithfulness, *Thy* righteousness standeth like the strong mountains." The ninth verse is one of the great expressions of all time.

ALGERNON HYDE VILLIERS

. . . Your accounts of the raids are deeply interesting. That we have to reprise is a bitter thing—another foul thing they have forced upon us.

It seems to me that sitting helpless in a house, with as much chance as anybody else of getting a bomb, must be about as trying a form of persecution as one can imagine. It is quite another story when you can think it is part of the natural course of affairs, and that all your surroundings have been arranged for such a situation.

Such a journey I had from Havre! A Belgian army motor was lent to Father for me to go to Amiens. Three breaks-down lost the train easily. There was nothing for it but to go on to X. The lights gave out; but a stray Yank was picked up who knew the way. We crept forward, often at a foot's pace, in the pitchy dark of the rain-stormy night.

When we did get to X. the light railway train had left! One more effort! I succeeded in stopping it, bringing the chauffeur up to one more groping *étape*, and at last he had done with me. . . .

When I got to the railhead I wandered long in the mud looking for the horses, but found them at last. But I forgot—the light train went off the lines! and I had to walk the last three miles with my awkward package of apples. A regular chapter of adventures, wasn't it? If I was glad to get in to a roaring fire and bed!

Things are quite jolly and comfortable here. " Recreational training " is the programme of an afternoon.

Think of me taking to Rugby football again! . . .

It is pouring outside. Am I not lucky to be able to sit in a jolly French kitchen with a high-perched blaze of logs ?

As I was coming back from the " furious sport," I met the T.O. and orderly, and we spoke somehow of jumps. He said there was one round the corner, and while he went in to see Jingle, I had both horses over. One couldn't jump a bit, and as there were no wings, we didn't make a great job of it. The other with a more Englishy shoulder was fine, and finally went sailing most willingly over the little rail. I was glad to find I was still *chez moi* in the saddle. Ah dear! how I love horses and what an expensive taste! Why isn't it gardening?

Here am I once more at my now quite familiar haunt in X. It is full of friends this evening. All my former hosts in the line turning up, full of greeting, and envy of my four days at Havre. Spirits are high, of course, as always on the move, and more especially when it is a move in the right direction. We go on to-morrow to a place near Arras. Most luckily we have had a perfect afternoon for our first *étape*. It was a little cold as we sat on the edges of open trucks, but the sky was of radiant clarity, and the views at moments really lovely.

We crossed the country evacuated by the Boche, and one well saw how it was our cavalry could do little in pursuit. There is nothing but wire, wire everywhere, great belts of it. Strange to say, there is as yet no sign of normal life returning to the precious fields. This place, however, has come on a good deal since my first visit, more than two months ago, and there are several shops of a sort open now. Félix Potin has straightened his board, and somebody is selling vegetables under it. The delight of the men at the faintest signs of civilised life is touching. They are such capital

121

fellows, and they do have to put up with very trying conditions. Before I went to Havre I invented a message of congratulation from Jingle which they liked, I expect.

Last night I began *L'Homme qui Assassina*. The pictures of Constantinople are exquisite, and I had the delicious smiling sense of going off into a vivid dream as I read. . . .

October 11th.

It is very jolly to have a day of complete calm to dispose of quite *à son gré*. Last night I began *Étapes et Combats*, and have just finished it. A wonderful little book. But the fantassin did not really care about his horses. There is one awful allusion to their sore backs, but never that *pre*occupation with their state, which must have filled our officers and men under a like ordeal. One puts the book down with a feeling of real reverence for every man who took the first shock of the Boche machine.

We shall never be called upon to do what they did, and one can hardly wonder that the Germans underestimated the strength of soul they had to meet. When Mallet becomes *fantassin*, and the scene is shifted to the trenches, the power and magic go out of the book to some extent, and again I can't quite forgive him for having left his regiment without a pang at parting from those faithful animals.

On this occasion I have been able to form a more adequate idea of X. As I walked the streets under last night's brilliant sky, the half-light hid the tattered condition of the houses, and revealed the fine width of the main street, and the dignified disposal of the surrounding masses of building. Out of the main street one is in a world of winding *ruelles*, slightly reminiscent of Cognac. They give their special note most clearly in a brilliant midday light, when the high walls cast deep shadows, and hold brilliant patches of colour. Most of the houses are brick of a fine dark colour. The church is a ruin, or nearly, though the western façade stands as a recognisable thing, with three unexploded shells stuck fast in the stones. I found the castle which I think M. associates with Charles Téméraire. It has three fat towers and an immense moat, but I wished I had known more of its history, in order to appreciate it better. The *hôtel de ville* is Renaissance, and has salamanders all over it, like the Château de François Ier at Cognac. It has been cruelly battered, but a fine frontal arcade remains, propped up with beams of a rare shade of colour—a sea-green tint in the grey of the stone. Under the salamanders is the inscription, " Nutrisco et extingo." Altogether it is a fine old place, and we have been very lucky to spend a glorious autumn day here. . . .

There is a recently-erected monument in the middle of the *Place*, a sculptured tablet is all broken to pieces —underneath it is the date 1536. Then on one side an inscription to "Catherine de Poix, surnommée Marie Foure, heroine du siège." Does this suggest anything to you ? My present enthusiasm for the French is lighted up by the sight of a pair of cherry breeches in the street to-day. I hope, but without much confidence, to see more of them these next days. I would so love to do a course on the 75's, or in some way or other to find contact with their martial mind.

La Herlière,
October 13th.

How much do you feel that religion with you is a " success " ? To my mind, as you know, that is a very important thing. Men have ceased to be afraid of God, and they won't abandon low standards and interests except for something which they can rationally call "better." As regards religion, the mass of men are not hypocrites to-day, are they ? They are waiting to be convinced. It is very much one's business to "prove all things" in these times ; and if Christianity stands the test, why should there not be a future for the reality of it ? It looks to me as if it were the one thing for which there were a future. . . .

But I have got so much to tell you of other things and to answer in your letters. Let me first describe our second *étape*.

We bustled off early to the station and sat there for three hours ! At last the train arrived.

The loading of the limbers was fun. Imagine a sloped bank about four feet high and as wide as an average road. The reverse side is steep-perpendicular, and up against it the end of a string of flat, open rail-way trucks is butted. The ends of the cars are lowered, and sleepers put on the buffers to fill the space between one car and another. Thus a straight road is made right down the train. A loading-party is told off beforehand. Up come the limbers at the trot to the top of the slope—Halt ! Unhitch the mules, and away they go to be boxed, while so many men take their place at the pole and hang on to the wheels, and the limber trundles away, bumping and heaving down the train causeway to the furthest end. We had a lot to get on, and the thing was done in under one minute per axle. That is the official way of reckoning. It rained a good deal at intervals. When we got into the train the weather settled into a downpour.

Coming along we played round games and sang, and were very amusing about the major and the real credit he was to the plumbing trade, so that the five hours of our tiny journey soon passed. When we got out it was dark, blowing a gale, and pouring. Nobody to meet us, or say what was to be done. We stood in the rain hoping the limbers might be shunted and left. Not at all. The brigade-major estimated we had a six hours' job to clear the train and get away! In three and a half from the time we came in, we were marching out of the station in high fettle, soaked (the men), and singing as I had not heard our company before. The men are really splendid, and to see them trundling the limbers and cook-carts and R.A.M.C. carts and all the rest of it away down the road with the rain drenching their khaki was a truly excellent thing.

The last effort of the day was a real stiff one. We had five miles to march to where we are now. The wind had got up to a regular gale, and beat the rain right into us marching against it.

We started at 10 p.m., so we had had no meal for some time. If I felt tired, what must they have felt like, with far more stuff to carry, and much more work to their credit.

The whole thing was positively weird, and I had a strange sensation of drifting on in an unknown element, and almost losing the sense of identity. However, it wasn't really far, though quite far enough. We got the men settled in at last, and issued a tot of rum to keep the cold out, and then R. and I got up to our billet and had a scrumptious feast. For the first time all your preparations for such an emergency came right in. First the turtle soup—delicious and boiling hot from the cooker. Then meat tablets, a Havre cake and cheese straws—choc. too, of course. We did enjoy it. Three o'clock saw us in bed at last, gloriously tired and happy, as one always is to have made an effort, and made good on it.

We are in a farm, and the farm is in a real village, unshelled though very tumble-down, with live French people in it, and seas of mud and manure!

ALGERNON HYDE VILLIERS

. . . I have gone on to Mark, which is ever splendidly sharp and vigorous. How quickly Christ and the Pharisees crossed swords ! He really almost seems to provoke them—at any rate, to challenge them.

I love hearing about the live stock and the trees. It is sad indeed about the poplar. They are so lovely out here ; standing in little groups or singly, or with other trees, they are always beautiful and fit the French landscapes everywhere. There is a lightness and pliant grace about them which is always taking my eye. This is a very lovely place. The camp is down a little wee lane, overhung with trees and beastly muddy, which branches off a second-class, which branches off a big main road. The men are in huts which have been put up in regular little "clos" with old fruit-trees and deep grass. It is some time since last they were used. Robinson and I are in luck. We are in the farm to which the "clos" belongs, quite near the camp. We have two nice attics with beds. When we came there was no mess arranged, but I soon fixed it with my landlady that we should have her *pièce*. This is convenient for all for its nearness to the men, but especially for R. and myself sleeping overhead. My French has come in most useful. . . .

But to return to the lane. As you go down the trees end, and it goes on—dry now—between pleasant cultivation on either side, with here and there a poplar patch. The valley is closed by the view of another wood with a windmill, and a bit of white building showing in front and in the middle of it. Marvellously pleasant to me. But my first sketch will be of the house seen from across the lane with high trees behind it. There is a *depth* about the village and its trees which is delicious, with the *width* of the cultivation. It is an oasis and desert effect. To understand my "depth" think of deep lanes, deep embowered buildings, deep grass, and, alas! deep muck !

October 15th.

. . . Jingle is a very curious creature. The first evening we were here, he very rightly made a speech after mess about the immediate future, and preparing to meet the winter—it lasted one hour. The word "appalling" and the phrase "baffles description" were used some 500 times, I should think, and the whole thing was delivered with a vehemence of tone and gesture quite unlike anything you could conceive. I was amazed; though I had often heard him jaw and jaw about his affairs, this terrible jobation on the war and the weather, and the men and the Hun, was wholly unexpected. It seems he has combined plumbing with temperance lecturing. I can believe it. He has a regular "ranter's" resources—rather horrible, for one feels all sense is lost in a torrent of sound, and that is an abject spectacle. The wildest confusion results. What he really thinks about anything can probably not be determined, as he can hardly be said to think at all. What he says is this sort of thing: "The British Tommy—*by God*—there's nobody like him on the face of the earth," and almost in the same breath, "*By God*, the swine, they'll let you down every bloody time." There it is—his powers of utterance and of working himself up by the sound of his own voice are unusual.

October 17th.

The inspiring call of Christ has sounded in —— once and for all, so that now and always His Kingdom has come in ——'s heart beyond questioning or recall. I suppose one may fail almost indefinitely to achieve in practice all that that implies, but the conviction that Christ is Lord is the sure stronghold of the spirit against which the floods may beat, yet it will stand firm.

127

This is the point of the Christian appeal, " Only be-lieve. He that cometh to me shall never hunger, and he that believeth on me shall never thirst."

How can we thank God enough for the revelation whereby we are growing in the supreme faith that this is true ?

I was reading my little Pascal book the other night, and I thought you would like this :

" Resolve—to do little things as if they were great things for the Majesty of Jesus Christ, Who does them in us, and Who lives our life : and to do great things as if they were little and easy because of His all-power-fulness." I should like to have the original for that and the other greatest saying, " Console thyself. . . . "

The absurdity of putting anything beside Christ's own institution is as clear to me as it is to you. No difficulties can really exist in such a case. It is only necessary to fix on the essential fact that here we have His one construction of the kind—His sole institution—and be faithful to that fact, and obstacles will be found to have disappeared. That is the sort of way in which God's omnipotence is true. In so far as we take Christ as our way and truth and life, we are more than conquerors. I find so much in the Psalms which faultlessly expresses this. For example, lxxxi, 9 to the end. After all, idolatry is still the great hindrance to the coming of the kingdom, and it still leads, as we see, " even weeping " to-day, to the same tragically stupid disaster, as it did in Hebrew history.

Gwatkin's sermons sound the sort of thing one longs for and rejoices in above all. I look forward intensely to reading them. Your quotations are most enhunger-ing.

About the French. Yes, their *grosses pertes* were constantly before the minds of those I met. But no mention of a separate peace was ever made, and my impression was exactly the contrary—one of a clear grasp that *en finir* was becoming a real possibility, and that to relax now were not disloyalty so much as utter folly.

I too heard of Kerensky in the palace with powdered footmen in white silk stockings, but not of doping. But one cannot understand Russians. All this may be all right, though it is so bitter for us to hear. . . .

I have had such a jolly ride this afternoon by myself on a pony that may almost have been intended for a saddle. The going was perfect, and I had some lovely canters on roadsides guiltless of drains—they were more fieldsides than roadsides. The landscape is very appealing. One is so deep *en campagne*—little fields carpeting the gentle slopes, little roads winding ill-defined among them, at some distance the long line of tree tops like candle flames, as strictly conventional as toy trees out of a farm box, which line some *grande route*, and in front and behind, to right and left, middle-sized masses of sepia-coloured woods hiding each its well-intentioned but slightly disarrayed village, which the steeple reveals at a distance. There is a combination of open airiness and of cosiness about the whole scene which may well command a passion. It is all pale, almost wan on an October afternoon, but very tender and touching.

On Sunday a very excellent padre came over in the afternoon, and after church parade R., the O.C., Divisional M.G. Co., and I stayed to a Communion. It is all one, *à trois* in a tin hut, and in such a setting as my Whitsun service in gorgeous Lincoln, God's presence is always the same.

Afterwards R. and I walked for an hour and held much converse on eternal things! He seems to me to have got to the root of the matter with a simpler view than my own. I have no doubt his will stand the test for him, though it could not for me. It

K   129

doesn't matter so much what you think about God, if you really know Him personally! On the other hand, some thoughts about Him are a barrier for many, I fancy, and better thoughts would help many to the essential knowledge.

October 18th.

We had a route-march to-day—such a lovely afternoon of sunshine and cool breeze.

I was in command, and thoroughly enjoyed the walk, not so much as my ride, of course, but still it is very satisfactory to me to get familiar with this corner of great France. The lightness of the trees' foliage is the great joy. Perhaps a few leaves may have fallen, but only quite a few. The transparency of the bushy tops is an exquisite feature, and here one has extraordinary variety of disposal. At the place where we halted to-day there was a group of three stems in front, perhaps 500 yards away—a picture of graceful loveliness in itself. Then to the left a *massif* pierced by the regular village spire and showing a high stockade of *élagué* stems, while to the right the long avenue line of a main highway stretched out of sight. Here and there a real yellow patch is coming, but for the most part the colouring is very neutral this year. The sense that I have of the landscape as a whole is that it is absolutely free from anything like meretricious, exciting, and ephemeral beauties, and that it asserts with extraordinary *authority* its own absolute value and fitness. It has the finest feminine qualities of quiet and of dignity, with a touch of mystery, expressed in the simplest and most gracious form. There is nothing heavy or magnificent, nothing bold or challenging, but an appeal as of something delicate, almost frail, an influence as of something assured and final, knowing all things and hoping all things. A very wise, mature country, patient and inwardly beautiful.

I hope my attempt to describe the indescribable will not be tiresome to you. It is rather fun to try and put words to what has been just sense as one looked and delighted.

I think the *Challenge* of October 12th is a bit flat. The Cuddesdon Sermon is no doubt calculated to soothe and smooth. But do you think all this oil on the water is really wise ? I feel rather Charley-esque [1] in face of so much placating on all sides. Love is the Christian ideal, but love is a passion, isn't it ? It is all rather Laodicean, and does make one feel rather spewy at moments. I miss Temple's freshness and vigour more than I can say. Fairness to other men's minds is frightfully important, but must that mean feebleness in the expression of one's own ? To distort other people's arguments, and even not to be genuinely interested in them and what is behind them—motive and character—is utterly wrong, foolish, and stultifying. The party point is nauseous. But I am all for a clear lead. There will be plenty of time to make concessions. But there should be something from which to concede.

Don't you think it is very poor of the note-writer to assume that we are not " in spirit aggressive " ? He is quite certain we should not be, and believes we are not. I rather think we should be, and hope that we are. I should say Christ and St. Paul and all great Christians are essentially aggressive. The Gospel is most intolerant. An easy-going attitude is worlds away from it. But it is an intolerance not so much of temper as of conviction—a clear-sightedness which insists on separating black and white, and refuses to rest in any attitude which obscures their difference— and above all, it is an unselfish intolerance. It is

[1] Charles Sydney Buxton, son of Viscount Buxton.

selfishness which defeats love. It is not amiability
which promotes it. Thus in the case of the war, I
think it is fair to say of the demand for victory that we
do not seek it to gratify an obstinate vanity, but because
the German national idea is a hideous outrage. " Il
faut en finir." " This practice must cease," as army
orders have it. It would be positively wicked to drop
our attitude of hostility in such a case, or look around
for some means of decently forgetting it.

I'm afraid all this is only too familiar, and too well
agreed between us to be very interesting. . . .

October 22nd.

When I was already fast asleep last night, our second-
in-command came and told me I was to go for the
day to Doullens for a jaunt.

Two of the nicest brother-officers came too, and I
have just got in from a very good day.

We started at 8 from Brigade H.Q., a few miles
away, so breakfast was ordered early, and failed to
appear. Our mess is run by the too inefficient padre.
He is the laziest, most useless individual I have ever
struck. He exercises no direct and practically no
indirect influence on our manners and customs, but
sits like a dough pudding smiling amiably at nothing.
Yet he has an intelligent face, and he has read a fair
amount. Supine is not the word for him.

The result of our late breakfast was a wild skirmish
along the hard high to Brigade. However, we arrived
in time with horses sadly heated. Fortunately it is
not far. Thence we lumbered in a motor-lorry to
the nice little " bourg." It is exactly that. . . . After
luncheon I went just out of the town and made a
sketch of the delicious *beffroi*. Tea and some pur-
chases for the mess, and a sleepy rumble home, brought
me to your letter. . . .

Yes, I am inclined to think my happiness does depend

on the clear realisation of the strength of the Spirit. As we bumped along our return journey this evening, I had a very decisive sense of the value of these things— the things of the Spirit.

The first great advantage which comes to me is, I think, " clarity." Grasping God's hand, I see things so much more steadily. " Be still and know that I am God" is a very true and suggestive thought. He seems to stop the boat rolling, as it were, so that one can see with' certainty how to steer. It is then a steering by the stars, isn't it ? He puts an end to our confusion of mind where, without Him, vanity, love of pleasure, laziness, conceit, and irritability, are alternately master. But His rule in the heart gives order, patience, power, serenity, and that deep sense of joy which one has in things being as they should be. It is not wholly a question of success or failure, but of poise which nothing can shake. . . .

The quotation, " Behold I stand at the door and knock," is surely the most deeply moving in all the New Testament. How precisely true it is ! As we vibrate to the pathos of it in the case of Christ's earthly life among those whose ears were so cruelly stopped against His message, so we must feel it of God's eternal life in relation to mankind. Such utter patience is a thing to dwell upon with deepest reverence. " Consider and bow the head." When at last we do listen to the sound we have really been wanting so long, what an example of the Divine method it is ! . . .

" Behold I stand at the door and knock." You could not find a more penetrating picture of the Divine, or one which gave more pointedly what seems to be the mark of the Divine—the Majesty of Spiritual might which belongs to the plainest externals. . . .

Well, no, I think active service on the whole makes it easier to be a Christian. The disturbance and publicity of which life so largely consists are against it, certainly, but on the other hand the need for God is great, and the clean and honourable life of a soldier is given you in exchange for the mean complacencies of a money-getting existence. There is less love in civil than in military life. Harry told me of the most heartfelt manifestations on his leaving Caterham. . . .

October 24th.

Please send me Gwatkin, if at all practicable. I feel certain he would be a continual inspiration. Not that I have been feeling " dry " just lately or unsustained. A few days ago, after I had been less regular than usual in making a nice time for mountaineering, I felt a sense of poverty in life most distinctly. It was a touch, but unmistakable, of all-over-the-place-ishness. The remedy is quite infallible, and for these last days I have had the happiest touch with the seen and temporal, by way of the unseen and eternal. It is lovely when one is going off to sleep to have no disordered or discontented mind, but one which the idea of Christ's goodness and greatness fills with a sense of security and benediction. It is very much like being well nourished in the spirit. " The Bread of Life " is a very apt phrase, I think. Christ comes into our lives under greater forms, no doubt, but the great occasions will, I should say, be best met by the soul which has been led every day to the green pastures and waters of comfort. . . .

ETAPLES,
October 26th.

We got here in time for an hour and a half's sleep, wash-up and breakfast. When I say " we," it includes a delightful lad of about twenty, who commands another company in the division. He was at Wellington, and went to Sandhurst when war broke out. He

134

is a very pleasant and they say a most competent fellow
—wonderful to think of his age.

We started along the road to Camiers hoping to
pick up a car of sorts. There was a perfect hurricane
of wind and sand, and after several disappointments,
and walking nearly halfway, we tumbled with intense
relief into an R.A.M.C. motor driven by a kindly
lady, and going just where we wanted to go.

The gale was really terrific and the sand for ever
filling one's eyes—a distinctly vexatious business.
However, the sunshine cheered us. I was glad to see
the fine downs, which were practically lost to view
in the incessant rain of my former days here.

There was a great gathering of notables for the
demonstration. The red hats must, I think, have
outnumbered the plain in a crowd of 200 or 300 men.
None of our heaviest were there, but a large assort-
ment of brigadiers and divisional commanders.
These were full of salutes for a minute Portuguee,
who must have been the G.O.C.-in-Chief we thought.
He was quite four feet high, and wore his green chin-
strap festooning his back hair. The general impression of the *omnium gatherum* from all our armies was
decidedly good. The cavalry were conspicuous—
they have an unmistakable air; lovely, spindle-legged
lads in soft leggings and distinguished-looking colonels
stopping their unaccustomed ears when the guns fired!
While we were waiting for the opening chorus I spotted
General Lawrence, looking handsome but battered.
His division is just out from the Ypres fighting.
He seemed fairly well and in good spirits, and was
most kind and pleasant during our few minutes'
chat.

Our own general was in great form, and threw out
some genial remarks in my direction. His table at
luncheon was positively uproarious. Altogether I
greatly enjoyed the human aspect of the occasion.

From the technical point of view it was interesting, instructive, and admirably stage-managed. . . .

I must prepare you for events in the near future. . . .

We expect to be in the thick of it before we are very much older. You will not be worried or anxious, I know, for your " heart standeth fast and believeth in the Lord." Ask His blessing on my efforts in new and surely difficult conditions. This great experience which I expect is coming will complete my training.

October 27th.

All the joy of four letters from you has been over-cast by the thought of those poor Buxtons. The account in the *Times* of yesterday by Denis's Eton contemporary is very touching to me, who have also had a Buxton friend. Denis need not have been Charley's equal to be a bitter loss to all who knew him. . . .

I liked Aunt B.'s sad saying, " French soil the finest for the dead." . . .

Jingle goes on leave to-day. . . . Last night we were talking to the R.C. padre about the visit of Cardinal Bourne to France, when J. from the other end of the table shouts out, " The Archbishop of York, he's the hell of a nut." I frankly guffawed. It appeared he meant the Bishop of London from his subsequent remarks. . . .

October 29th.

Yesterday I was suddenly whipped off on my new job. I had not far to go, but an awful long time before I could start work. In fact it was too late to do much, so I had to be very early this morning. Everything fitted in beautifully, and I have been much touched and pleased by the cordiality of everybody on my first performance. They accuse me, with only very slight reason, of unselfishness, and the happiness that gives me is worth anything. There is a look in men's faces sometimes which is the wonderfullest recompense for any amount of trouble.

I must repeat again that my warning was premature. I am sorry I sent it, for in this case "premature" may so well mean "entirely mistaken."

If I am cryptic, it is because I am afraid to be anything else. . . .

It is a fine thought—a country one has "marched over and fought for." I am so glad you liked my attempt to convey its rare quality. It has looked lovely to-day, the trees quite turned, but not very brilliant, and great rain-storms charging across the sky. The church has got its steeple cross bent right over, playing at being Albert.

A "clos"—how convey the expressive word?—is primarily an *enclosure*, but to me it has a significance of something small, cosy, withdrawn, and intimate.

SOMBRIN,
October 31st.

I gather the harvests here are good. I am always asking, and the reply is invariably cheering.

You can guess the latest idiotic rumour—we are for the Julian front!

Yes, the padre is R.C. and exceedingly indolent. However, I have had two very good talks with him lately. The first was in the nature of an argument, and I found him more utterly R.C.-ish than I had expected. I was quite taken aback to find that he believed in the Garden of Eden and the Fall story of Genesis as being substantially true. Altogether I felt R.C.-ism was impossible. But this evening after tea we went for a walk together, and I found to my great delight that he is also a Christian. It took a long time to rouse him from a rather lethargic general conversation frame of mind, but I succeeded at last,

and I intensely enjoyed the walk home. We discussed
Christ and Peter and Paul, and got well warmed up,
and I found that he really loved them, and we were
entirely at one.

I am interested in St. Mark, but rather as a study
than an inspiration. I look forward to another dose
of Paul before long.

October 31st.

The French victory is truly great, isn't it? There
seems to be a conciseness about their efforts which we
do not quite equal. On the other hand, one must
admit with sorrow that the Germans have got in a
good blow against ever valorous Cadorna. It is
astonishing that they have resources sufficient for an
attack on such a scale. We have not got to the bottom
of them yet. Their power of cohesion is a remarkable
thing when one remembers their long history of dis-
union and internal conflict, but I remain unimpressed
by it in my heart of hearts. The low level of the
whole thing makes the actual achievement almost
worthless. . . .

There is indeed with me a feeling that real life is
only going to begin when this peculiar dream is over.
It is not too bad a dream just now. Jingle's absence
leaves us a very harmonious party.

I have been much interested in the new work with
the artillery we have been doing. My wet days at
Camiers in August enable me to take the lead in this,
and I have enjoyed the lecturing and drilling involved.
It is always fun to bring order out of chaos in the
men's minds and on the parade-ground. The only
drawback is the beastly cold and the shortage of fuel.
The latter is really most trying. I go for a good walk
along the road, before going to bed, to warm up. However, things will be better to-morrow. R. and I have
a nice big empty room in which we have our sleeping-

bags spread on wire beds of the usual order. I could not stand up in my former *gîte*, but here I actually Müller in the mornings. The brick floor and black-beamed ceiling are rather jolly, and when Harrison has fixed me up a table I shall be admirably placed. The village is gathered round its church very pleasantly, and, as usual, is deep in trees.

The mules have a delicious " clos," and the horses a stable just next door to me, so that I can go and see them at any minute, which I do, with some enjoyment. There is a theatre just exactly like the drill-hall at E. Linton, and we had the usual awful concert last night. It is a great thing, though, when it rains and for lectures. . . .

The beliefs so precious to us and so hard to spread are easy to ridicule, and yet sorely needed on every hand. I found myself composing a sort of credo this morning. . . .

November 1st.

There has been no mail to-day. . . . Whatever the reason, I am letterless. That is always sad, and this evening an idiotic sing-songing or song-bawling mood overtook the young lads after dinner and bored me rather heavily. So I feel a little depressed. Nothing, however, is more refreshing and cheering than to sit down for an hour's chat with you. It is hard on those who are not married, and married as you and I are, so that they really lift one another above the transitoriness of the common world into the timeless world of eternal verities. I find that idea —that we can discover here and now in various ways a road from the fugitive and unsatisfactory into the eternal " now "—most consoling. Temple's *Mens Creatrix* gave it to me, and I have proved it very true. What a significant fact it is that an idea is, if true, only a vision of what was true before, but yet, by being

139

stated and brought home to one, it actually creates something new for one. The fitness of the name *Mens Creatrix* is very well illustrated in this.

As I talked with the padre last night, I was very conscious of the absurdity of sectarian differences. They rest on such trivial issues—trivial, at any rate, in comparison to the unifying convictions. I found that when it was a question of the special value of the fact of Christ, or of the reason that made so many neglect that precious fact, or of the delight in St. Paul, or of the significance of prayer and sacrament, or apparently any of the things which really matter to the inner man, the R.C. and I were brothers, rejoicing in one another. The love we felt for Christ, faint enough I dare say, was yet strong enough to constrain us really to love one another. This must be the most beautiful and the most hopeful fact in the world—that there is this wonderful Being Whose magic Personality—once we are really interested in Him—unites, uplifts and rejoices all sorts and conditions of men. When we are together again, let us not forget to make the effort—happy and delightful in itself—of meeting one another more and more in Him.

I take it there is nothing obscure or mystical about this except in its results. It is simply the taking an interest in Christ, reading and thinking about Him, and coming to care about Him and to grow fond of Him, just as we might study and grow devoted to some lesser historical figure, that leads perhaps in the end to the fullness of God. The method is quite commonplace, the result quite obvious and to be expected. It is in the *quality* of the result that we see with whom we have to do. . . .

I am sorry (a little) that the Omnipotence correspondence is closed, for L.M. puts us back at just the misleading angle that I was seeking to get away from.

When she speaks of God deliberately willing sin with so much horror, she is thinking of Him as outside the world and responsible (or not), as it were, for what happens in it. Whereas, if I am right, God is in His world facing the necessity of sin, and for ever redeeming it, by working it into the triumph of goodness, till we all come to a perfect man, far greater by our sins than any mere innocence could make us. There must be some meaning in, " There is more joy in Heaven over one sinner that repenteth"; and God's ways of redeeming the sins of the world are far more various and inscrutable than the single way of repentance in the individual heart.

Christ's triumph did depend upon the exceeding sinfulness of the Jews, and so we may be sure that God is not mocked. He is not worsted by our wrongdoing. He knows how to use it all.

Do you know the famous saying, " O felix culpa quae tantum et talem meruit habere Redemptorem " ? Is it an outburst of St. Augustine's ? It is, in any case, 'a thing to keep in one's mind waiting for the full illumination of it to reach the level of complete consciousness.

I have just re-read this, and wonder how I could have been so faithless as to mention my mood at starting. I really knew quite well that I should have to unsay it before I had gone very far. It seems worlds away now. . . .

The Italian news is rather awful, isn't it ? Strength of soul ! We aren't going to win easily even now. But what times to live in ! Immense in their terror and challenge.

November 2nd.

I go unrefreshed by a letter . . . once more to-day. However, I am in high spirits, having played a capital, mud-larking game of football this afternoon.

141

One feels extraordinarily good all over after that most remarkably excellent sport. We, with some help from the Divisional M.G. Co., are playing the Brigade to-morrow, and expect to have an almighty tough fight of it.

Provided you use some familiar phrases, you can get a hearing, at least from our thoughtless people, for almost any nonsense or wrong. In consequence of meeting with this horrible idea, I find myself being much more pro-Russian than I had been. With all their tragic folly and incapacity, they are still a thousand times nearer to us than the man-eating ants of Prussia.

I was cheered by Smuts's cool, firm speech on Italy.

All Saints' Day was very real and happy to me. A great deal of attention was paid to it in the village, as everywhere in France, I think. The bell of the church has a beautiful note. It seemed to be summoning the parish at all hours.

I have such a delicious reminder of Finedon from my room. I look out on to the tall spire at just the same angle and from just the same distance. The window itself, too, is of the Finedon proportion, and has a smaller part at the top which doesn't open, and a double light below opening down the middle. That is right, isn't it? Of course, the dear little panes are not there, and the tiled spire is as unworthy as you like to be compared with the perfect spring of the red and grey at Finedon. Still, it has been enough to remind me of all the beauty, dignity, and peace, which belonged to that cherished spot.

There are two delightfully French trees at the edge of the churchyard which I greatly enjoy, and am always intending to sketch. . . .

I wish I had time to arrange my theologico-seraphic fancies into a series of papers. I should like to straighten them all out into a consecutive view of the whole great subject. Perhaps, however, that will come later, and will be better worth doing with fuller knowledge.

It has been a warm, drizzling day, by no means unpleasant, rather comfy in fact. I do hate a penetrating wind. This is my fourth month in France, and twelfth of foreign service. What luck I have had ! . . .

November 4th.

I am afraid I allowed the sense of discomfort and stuffiness to creep into my letter of yesterday. I am so sorry. Things are very different to-night. I have been for a very jolly ride this afternoon, and am now established in the room occupied by two " of ours," with table and chair and fire—the acme of cosiness. . . .

I was thrilled by your mention of Cyrano on the leaves. Can I quote the lines ? *Je crois bien.*

> " . . . Comme elles tombent bien
> Dans ce trajet si court de la branche à la terre.
> Comme elles savent mettre une beauté dernière,
> Et malgré leur terreur de pourrir sur le sol,
> Veulent que cette chute ait la grace d'un vol.'

They are indeed favourites—a wonderful swinging movement about them, like nothing outside Hardy on the trees. . . .

I have written a *Challenge* letter about sin, suggested by L.M.'s letter in answer to mine, and founded on what I wrote to you two nights ago. I long to see a determined effort to get to the facts on these and the other great problems of life. There is no more insidious devil than the one that suddenly sends a feeling, more than a thought, into one's consciousness, that the religious position is a piece of hocus-pocus—all right for certain moods, but not real life—not workable fact. I know him at once and can deal with him, but I see what a real devil he is, and what an immense amount of material he has to his hand in the second-rate thinking and practice of Christianity. Christ, on the other hand, completely bowls him out every time, and gives one the exactly opposite sense that only through the unseen and eternal can we cope with the seen and temporal.

It is still warm and muggy—the mist very thick, but I rather enjoy this, as you know. I am now definitely recommended for second-in-command, and warmly congratulated. . . .

. . . I haven't any news, and I must tell you that I shall probably seem very jejune on soldiering.

Heavy warnings keep coming out on " Leakage " of information.

One cheerful detail (of which the Boche could not possibly make any use) is that I am splendidly well!

A lady of the village is contemplating a claim against Charlie Clay's department, " pour la *dégradation* de ses herbes." Isn't that nice—the degradation of the herbs ? I have been reading your Tolstoy. It is charming, but his idea of Christianity is *outré*. He is a finer writer than thinker, I should say. I wonder if that strange people may recover at all during the hibernation of the next months. The figures of the captures of guns and M.G.s by the French impressed me profoundly this morning. They are really marvellous. I find the more intelligent here manage to un-British themselves enough to be acutely admiring of them.

November 6th.

Very good news to-day, as the Arab paper-boys used to say—Jingle is not coming back. We believe his successor is a very good fellow.

We played football again to-day. I'm sure I played futilely, but it was great fun, and makes one feel very beatific, though slightly tired. Another game is in prospect to-morrow, so I am doing well for exercise. That is all my news, so I will turn to your letters. Yes, your weather is evidently much better than ours. We don't have great downpours, but the ground is thoroughly soaked, and the air simply full of moisture.

I am taking advantage of the kindness of M. le Curé, who lets us use a little warm room of his next his kitchen, where he sits with his sister and mother. It is usually rather full, but to-night there is a boxing competition in our drill-hall, so everybody has gone over there.

Having no Bible with me prevents my answering you in detail about the Psalms. I agree in a general way about the wicked, but have I never told you how I habitually, and now almost unconsciously, interpret those passages ?

They stand for me, those wicked, for all the " evil thoughts which may assault and hurt the soul." I find in nine cases out of ten there is not the slightest diffi-culty in so understanding the words. It is also perfectly natural that some such interpreting should be necessary, for the evils of different ages are not the same. The way to meet them, however, does not change. That is why the Psalms are immortal poems, for they give the sovereign rule of life in unrivalled simplicity and beauty of form. " Seek His face ever-more"—that is the way to tackle whatever oppresses the human soul. " I have set God always before me " —that is the way in all ages that the true greatness of life is revealed in thought and in action.

As the world goes on, the enemy will be ever more subtle, but not less strong maybe, and we shall still need the Psalms to sound again in our hearts the war songs of God's primitive chosen.

One cannot too eagerly long that our enemies, the haters of the Lord—the things against God in life, the God who is in us, our best self, the hope of our glorified future—that such shall come into slippery places and, falling down, disclose their instability.

The "stability" of Christ—that was a fine word of yours. I see the Archbishop's sermon was on "Jesus Christ the same yesterday, to-day, and forever," but with ever new worlds to conquer and to subdue, till we all come in the fullness of time unto a perfect man to the measure of the stature of the fullness of Christ. Glorious words! To transcribe them is a religious act, and the eloquence of St. Paul is not an easy-flowing thing, wherein subject is a mere content of form: it is the upstruggling into speech of the things too wonderful and excellent for me, but the truest, most precious things of all.

Well . . . I have got a lot of men's letters to censor, as I am orderly to-day, and get H.Q. as well as the section to do. H.Q. men are very verbose too—so I will stop and wish you good night.

November 8th.

I did not write to you yesterday, I am sorry to say. My day was very full. The morning was occupied with the troops. After luncheon we had a conference to consider the field-day, from which I have just come in. I then hurried over to Har,[1] and got back just as a show by the divisional entertainers was opening. I felt I must throw myself into this, though it was not too good to be missed by any means. . . .

I liked seeing Harry very much . . . had been thrilled by the accounts given by his local *maire* of all the political devilries which centre in Caillaux. . . .

The only man who could cope with Caillaux seems to have been old Galliéni, who placed him under arrest in the early days for clamorously demanding

---

[1] Captain H. Graham.

an interview when the General was busy with other things. . . . The *maire*, who is royalist and Catholic, says that before the war all moral sense had been abandoned or lost in France, but that the war was bringing it back. He lost a Government inspector-ship when he entered his son at a Jesuit school, and has a story of General Castelnau, who thought it necessary to explain that he had a Jesuit brother when some post was offered him, lest he should be thought to have taken it under false pretences.

The field-day has been rather feeble, confused, and fatiguing, not a success, I should say. Our new C.O.[1] is a capital fellow as far as I can see, very conscientious and keen. A serious person, at any rate. I'm sure he is not simply *pour rire*, like his predecessor. The situation in Italy is certainly terribly anxious. One does so dread a desecration of Castelfranco, Venice, Padua, and the places that we and so many thousands have so ardently loved. The news of Wm. Temple is very good and fine.

To M. V.

November 9th.

Thank goodness, human beings are actually far more elastic than a great many who have never been stretched can bring themselves to admit. It is good to be stretched and establish one's elasticity, isn't it ? . . .

This country is most beautiful. The villages are hidden in trees and betrayed by their *flèches* alone. There are any number of them, joined by little wet roads between the open fields. It attracts me strongly. It has an air of authority and dignity which is more affecting than the picturesque. One feels at once it is a Mother earth. . . .

[1] Major S. G. Davey. Killed March 23rd, 1918.

There was an account of Denis Buxton in the *Times* which recalled Charley. Though I hardly knew Denis, I felt his death for what it reminded me of. I have never yet met anyone I admired and liked so much as Charley. He had a very rare combination of spiritual, intellectual and social gifts. I often wonder what he would have done in the war. Been killed, I suppose, to a certainty.

We are thoroughly enjoying these times, but the winter is a terrible prospect, especially for those who have been through one.

November 9th.

. . . The more I see of our new C.O. the more I like him. He is full of energy, and no " eye-wash " man at all. I am sure he knows his job and is wrapped up in it. . . .

It is a joy to have such a man for a C.O. . . .

I had a long talk this morning with M. le Curé. He spoke faultlessly-chiselled sentences of really expressive richness on the great topics of Christ and His place in life. I loved to hear him. When we came to the things that divide, I found a stone wall behind his handsome, animated features.

He admitted that a sincere Protestant, though in error, is *de bonne foi,* and may be saved. I asked him why, if this were so, it was quite certain that all the truth was on his side, all the error on mine, if we were both sincere. He said that they were quite certain of the whole truth being with them, because of the Apostolic Succession. I was horrified, and said I could not understand how, in questions of such magnitude, a mechanical fact (doubtful in itself historically, I fancy) could be made to carry such weight. We parted very good friends, but I was grieved at his intransigeance. He is a splendid man to look at, young, tall and beautifully turned-out in cassock and hat caught up on each side. His beard is most elegant, and his bright brown eyes full of expression. If only our clergyman could look like him, have half his facility of speech and a liberal mind into the bargain! That is too much to hope for. It is a great thing, however, that our worthy men are not trained in his rigid mould. It is a paltry thing at bottom, that fixity of statement. One cannot believe it is quite fully sincere. It smells second-hand.

To Charles

November 8th.

. . . We have had a field-day to-day. Uncle Har was one of the umpires, and looked very fine on his big horse and with his bright red tabs and brassard. We all got rather wet in the morning, but got dry again by the afternoon.

It is great fun when we move from one position to another. I blow my whistle and wave my arms round and round, and immediately all the men jump up and carry off the guns and the tripods, and the ammunition, and all the things they have, and pack them like lightning into the limbers, which are like boxes on wheels. Then crack go the whips, the men scramble up somehow on to the limbers, and the good little mules go galloping off as fast as they can till I stop them, and everybody and everything tumbles out again, and a new position is taken from which to fire. We don't really fire on field-days, which make things a little bit silly, but all the same it is great fun.

I like the real firing best, especially when you see the horrible Germans fall or scuttle for shelter, as we often could see them when we were in the line. I must stop now. . . . .

149

Can you imagine what our feelings were when the door was blown in last night (when we were at dinner) by no other than Jingle himself? We spent anxious hours till all was made clear this morning and his orders to proceed to —————— duly arrived.

It has at any rate given us an increased sense of the excellent fortune which has befallen us in his departure. However, it is only fair to mention that he was most complimentary to me. . . .

It is a pity that one cannot value his good opinion in the very least. I don't think I ever met such a buckram person all round. . . .

· Yes, it does seem absurd to empty the church for the Lord's own service, and to fill it in order to hear a timid curate discoursing from the pulpit. Mattins followed by Communion is the worst possible arrangement. . . .

November 11th.

I am waiting for Hum [1] to turn up. He was to have been here by twelve o'clock, but it is now nearly two, and there is no sign of him. It will be a great blow if he doesn't come.

The news is as bad as even he could expect, isn't it? One really requires all one's fortitude to contemplate the conquest of Venetia and the final *pourriture* of Russia under Lenin. How long shall we and the French be able to keep loyal in the midst of so much collapse? I don't really doubt that we both shall be able to hold on, but this winter will evidently be a time of supreme strain and testing.

The *curé* here speaks of his countrymen just as one has been led to think of them.

[1] Captain Humphrey Paul.

150

He dwelt on the coldness of their clear vision, and the strength which that brought them.

He is a royalist and has a touching faith in the value of monarchical institutions. He is as rigid about politics as he is about religion. Except for the pleasure of his speech, he would not be very interesting company.

As it is, I am looking forward to his dining with us to-morrow. It will be a strain on our conversational powers, but I have imported an infantryman who is pretty fluent, and have hopes, too, that the C.O. will be able to support me. . . .

November 13th.

Another miss yesterday was greatly regretted by me, but was quite unavoidable. We were off early, and had a long march to a range among lovely dark woods.

It was a perfect day, dark and warm, and our road ran along a beautiful valley with steep, tree-clad sides, and through a jolly old town, the feature of which is an archway with a high building and a steep brown roof over it. The dignity of the little place and the radiant quiet of its surroundings put the war a very long way off. We had a most successful time on the range. My section remains in for the final in an M.G. competition to take place before the Brigadier, and my sergeant, by excellent rifle shooting, looked like doing us great credit in that line. . . .

To-day we have won the brigade cross-country run, one of our officers coming in first. This gives the greatest satisfaction to all, and is of real importance to our position in the brigade. Such things count for a lot, not altogether absurdly, I should say, and it is our great object to make the M.G. Corps the name it should have.

I was out with the C.O. this afternoon, and liked him

very much. We were doing a little professional stunt, and I greatly admired his imaginative good sense. His keenness and good manner make him entirely satisfactory. . . .

The *curé's* coming was a great success. He was just as I have described him, and harped on the same themes. We talked of books a little. He has read nothing but French literature. His detestation of the Republic and of democracy knows no bounds. I greatly enjoyed his beautiful speech and fine presence. He has gone back to be an R.A.M.C. sergeant to-day. His going has brought about an event of which you will love to hear. His room is occupied by the C.O. and R., and I have moved into the one in which I slept the first night I was here, likewise in the *presbytère*. I am writing in it now at a nice solid table, with the white sheets of my bed just visible out of the corner of my eye. It has the warmth of an inhabited house about it, which is good. We are now in clover, though the other place was not bad at all really. It was larger than this, had two nice windows, and was on the ground floor. The cold and absence of furniture were, of course, great drawbacks. I am glad indeed of the change. . . .

Daily duty surely comes first in the general laying-out of one's time and efforts. I can't believe God's will is that one should be inefficient. But nothing should stand in the way of a daily meeting with God, and that for purely practical, if for no other reasons. I am orderly officer to-morrow, and I'm sure I shall not do my job as well as I might if I do not take good care to allow for a time to be alone with our Father which is in heaven. The more anxious and difficult the work to be done, the more essential it is to get the spiritual succour needed to see it through. Orderly officer is a very small job out here—I only took it as an example of a very ordinary kind. The trouble is to do well whatever there may be to do without seeking God's help. . . .

I feel I am on the rock when I am, with Pascal, conscious of the Majesty of Christ in the small sphere, and looking to His all-powerfulness should I be called to a greater. This way one is happy in the present and for the future.

I must stop now. I have got to make some arrangements for a field-day to-morrow, and am going out to dine with the infantry. . . .

Wingy's [1] death made me quite sick to hear of for a moment. It is profoundly melancholy. How and when was it? There is nothing to do, in the face of the long succession of tragedies, but to bow the head. But it is *navrant*.

November 15th.

Yesterday an extreme form of field-day was suddenly sprung upon us.

We had to get up at four in the morning, and do a goodish march to the *champ d'exercice* before starting the proper activities of the day. These were quite strenuous, and we did not get home till 6 o'clock. Who should I find but Harry come to pay me a visit? He was very genial and cheerful, and made himself at home in our uncomfortable and unfamiliar surroundings, till I had some tea and brought him over here to chat for a little time till he went off home.

My new job comes into play again to-morrow, but it will cause me no trouble at all, as the ground to be dealt with is already perfectly familiar. . . .

I must really apologise for my flow of theology. I was positively overflowing with it about ten days ago.

Apropos of M.'s comment on my conference letter, I wonder whether (in the line of Wells's argument)

[1] Lieutenant W. Stuart was, happily, not killed, but a prisoner.

we have not passed the stage where individuals can really dominate, and must not be prepared to face the more difficult method of advance by means of general raising of the intellectual and spiritual level. . . .

The idea of a Russian's idea of madness is indeed portentous. Could they mean what we call "sane"? But really I am sorry for them, and hate to hear them abused, and the same with the Italians. Think how awful it would be for us if our armies and Government got into such a frightful condition. . . .

November 16th.

The duties of the "new job" were quite successfully carried out this morning. Everybody was most genial, even "affecting," and there were no difficulties of any kind.

There will be another similar venture to-morrow. Meantime the "depth" has, if anything, increased, especially as regards the muck. The excellent table Harrison fixed up for me remains intact, and I am writing from it now. He is an excellent old bird, but I hear from R. that the C.O. "ticked him off" heavily this morning for having a dirty tunic and long hair. Poor old thing, he has been chasing the company barber ever since, in spite of having been inoculated yesterday. It will be my turn soon, I expect. That is all my news!

I am sorry to think that —— should feel quasi-agnostic. I agree, of course, that the fullness of God is a mystery. But, though He is wrapped in mystery, He is surely not lost in it. Does she really feel that one cannot be sure of anything about Him? That seems to me to be a melancholy position, and not really in accordance with facts. However, perhaps it is beside the mark to say that, since the only relevant facts are facts of one's own experience, and these will be different in different cases. But then, again, that

is true of everything or anything which is commonly
called a fact.

So here we run right up against the vital question :
Can we have knowledge of God at all comparable to
our knowledge of one another ? It seems to me that
everything turns on this. A vague surmise, an eternal
question, is worlds away from a work a day piece
of common knowledge. Do you think you could try
and tell me what would be your own answer to this
question ? I will try and tell you something about
mine.

I feel perfectly sure of one thing—the foundation
of all the rest—that there is available for our constant
use an unseen source of personal power. That to
me is a fact like a table or chair, only, as the Dean
would say I think, more unshakable than the tables
and chairs. This is the fact of God. It is no good
saying that it is a piece of self-deception, for this
reason : that this fact of God stands on exactly the same
level as the fact of self. It goes through all experience
from top to bottom, and throughout its length and
breadth. It is in essence the same fact as that of self,
and one, clearly, cannot be self-deceived on the fact
of self. If self itself is a fraud, then there is no self
to deceive or be deceived. In other words, the whole
of experience falls to the ground. The fact of God
likewise, once grasped, is ultimate. You cannot over-
throw it and leave anything standing at all.

I have received a measure of power to live in the
fullest sense, and I have not received it from any
visible or tangible source. I don't think it is possible
·for me to be argued out of this. I come back to this
fundamental thing whenever I am tempted to doubt,
and there it is staring me in the face. I cannot get
away from it. The means to this knowledge is mainly,
almost wholly, indirect contact with the historical
Christ, which convinces me that in Him we have the

expression of that power which was, and which is, the spring of veritable manhood.

These are deep thoughts, but the experience is very elementary. It is hard to capture God, and enclose Him in a sentence, but it is also quite impossible, if He shows Himself to you, to avoid seeing Him. . . .

Now I must turn to more easily-handled matters, or it will be food time before I have answered your letter. . . .

Yes, I was much struck by the letter to Lord Rothschild. I feel it will be intensely interesting and helpful to us to have the Jewish people re-established as a political entity. I am quite glad Wells's Bishop is trashy. . . .

November 18th.

I did not write to you yesterday, as my day was very full. My work went off very satisfactorily, and I really enjoyed it!

Alas! I had no letter from you, and again none to-day.

The weather is wonderful—rather misty in the mornings, but very dry for the season, and with gleams of sunlight now and then. It is not anything like as cold as it was in Scotland this time last year. I remember the icy keen afternoons, and the long evenings spent in absorbing St. Paul and writing to that absurd " Active Service." The fall seems to be my composing season, doesn't it?

One great advantage, I notice, is possessed by religious novelties and side-shows. They are quite easy to confess. There is no difficulty about saying, " I am not afraid of being shot, because I am a Christian Scientist." It is extremely difficult to say that one is a Christian, and there is no other way of saying that one is seeking to follow Christ. Unfortunately, the word Christian has become so closely associated with moral perfection that one cannot call oneself the former without appearing to lay claim to the latter. It is offensive, and indeed absurd, to say, " I did this, or feel so, because I am a good man," isn't it ? But that's what one will be understood to mean by saying one is a Christian. I want some way of saying that . I believe in Christ without implying that I am like Him, just as Harry can believe in Mrs. Eddy without suggesting that his literary sense has forsaken him ! Perhaps I shall find a way before long ; one usually does by being patient.

Last night I was taken to task again for the way I had done this job, and I longed to be able to say, " Of course I did the thing that way—it is the only sensible way to do things," remembering " the words of the Lord Jesus, how He said . . ."

It seemed such a chance to set forward His cause when people were touched, and I was so entirely solid and happy. However, it seems that it was not to be. I felt as if I was restrained. I expect when I have more fully tested the power that worketh in us, and proved beyond any possibility of doubt that it is the Lord, then I shall be able to witness to it.

It looks to me as if that time must soon be coming. After all, I have lived by His light for over a year now, with the torch burning away in the pitcher, only showing through chinks to the nearest at hand, and soon the signal ought to come to break the pitcher and blow the trumpet, and shout for the Sword of the Lord. Perhaps it never will. It is in God's hands. I feel no fear of heavy trials, no doubt which is the rock on which to build a safe and happy house. I read glorious Joshua i 1–9 yesterday. Nearly twenty years ago Bull set the text on the fly-leaf of the little book I am using still. It is a supreme passage, none finer in the Old Testament. . . .

ALGERNON HYDE VILLIERS

Yes, I alluded to vicarious suffering (in letter of November 1st). That does seem to be a fact, strange though it is, and the important thing is to try and stick to the facts, and not fit them into the ideas of what we should like to be true.

It is growing rather cold these days, isn't it ? And a brazier of wood makes such an infernal smoke that it is hardly worth having it. . . .

Impossible write more now, too much interrupted.

From Major S. G. Davey

—— MACHINE-GUN COMPANY.

You will probably know that I have only been with the company some three weeks, but during that time I had seen a good deal of your husband, and we were beginning to form a friendship which I hoped would be very close. As an officer, no words are too good for him, he was so extremely thorough and efficient : his whole heart was in his work, and his loss is a very great blow to all of us.

Two days before he died we went for a long walk, and he told me of you . . . ; he talked, too, of his hopes for later on, when the social problems come to be solved, and of the share he wished to take in their solving.

His influence in the company was splendid : as you know, we have many boys of nineteen or under serving in the army, and he was excellent with these younger ones.

He died in full health and spirits, shot through the head by a sniper. There could have been no pain. He was going forward ahead of his men to reconnoitre.

Later on, at dusk, I went up near the spot myself. It was a hillside with longish rough grass : on the right there was a big wood, from which the hill sloped down.

A flock of mallard flew across the sky just before dark, and I thought that he would have liked that : he was very fond of birds.

Despite the fact that there was a good deal of rifle-fire going on, and some shelling, there was a kind of peacefulness over everything, and he himself was very peaceful. . . .

You must have a realisation that he was ready to go on to other work, and I am perfectly sure that that was so.

Letter from the Subsection Officer

The day before we went into action the C.O. had the details of the attack given him, and decided that one section should go over the top behind the last wave of infantry, to help them in case of need, and to consolidate the objectives in turn, as they were won. The remaining three sections, it was arranged, should stay behind to do barrage work.

The C.O. at once decided that No. 2 Section should be the one to go with the infantry, which was a great honour, and compliment to the section in general, but to your husband in particular, as he was in command of it, and the work it was called upon to do was much more dangerous and difficult than the task of the other sections, and demanded much greater leadership on the part of the man in charge. It is only fair and right to say that his section was undoubtedly the best, and deserved this distinction, and it was all through his zeal and energy that the section was so good. The men would have followed him anywhere, under any conditions.

At 10.30 on the 23rd the attack started, and our four guns followed about 400 yards behind the last wave of infantry. For the sake of co-operation and liaison with the infantry, we decided that your husband should stay all the time with the last infantry wave, while I followed behind with the section. Our first objective was a ridge on the left of Bourlon Wood, and just outside it, known as " 100 Spur " ; and our second, Bourlon village and the high ground beyond.

All went well as far as the first objective, and the brigade on our right, which attacked the wood, seemed to be going well. We were held up by machine guns at " 100 Spur" (the Boche machine guns were very numerous, and he put up a very effective barrage with them, though he had no artillery to speak of), and your husband came back to help me to get the guns into action, to try and help the troops in front to advance.

I was hit in the thigh as we were doing this, and he turned to me and shouted, " Hard luck!" as a farewell message, for, of course, in a show like this, once a man is wounded no more notice can be taken of him by the people who are advancing. My last view of your husband was of him directing the guns' fire and encouraging his men in face of a pretty deadly fire, and I think it is a picture of him of which you may well be proud. I can tell you I was.

On my way down to the dressing-station, a man overtook me with a message from him to the C.O., so I know that he was all right for at any rate half an hour after I got hit. I heard a rumour of his death at the dressing-station about five (I was hit about noon), but I kept on hoping against hope till I saw his name in the casualty list.

I would like to tell you once more how very dear his friendship was to me. He came to us in August, and I was appointed subsection officer under him almost at once. . . .

Your husband, by his unbounded zeal, and tireless

energy and keenness, made us see that things were worth doing well, and it was through him more than anyone else that, when we went into action on the 23rd, we were a company to be proud of, and our section was one of which I will be proud to my dying day.

The officer commanding the infantry company wrote :

We soon came under fairly trying enemy artillery and machine gun fire.

Mr. Villiers' work was particularly arduous, and consisted chiefly of moving his guns about to deal with isolated enemy posts.

In spite of the fact that he was forming a good target for enemy snipers and machine guns, Mr. Villiers moved calmly about the field directing his battery, and I know that he successfully put one, if not two, enemy posts out of action, and prisoners were brought back.

He walked about with cigarette and walking-stick, and his cheerfulness and remarkable coolness must have inspired his men.

PAPERS READ TO MACHINE-GUN PUPILS,
JANUARY—FEBRUARY, 1917

ENGLAND, certainly Scotland, is called a
Christian country; and though perhaps we
cannot see anything very Christ-like in our
common way of life in these islands, it is at any rate
true that most of us have at one time in our lives had
the wish to make something real and practical of the
Christian religion. We should all be quite glad if we
could find out something about that religion which
would make it of use to us and make us proud of it.
I admit this is not a strong justification of our calling
ourselves a Christian people. In ordinary times it is
not enough to make us overcome our habit of lazily
accepting things as they are, and ask whether, behind
the absurdity of clergymen's clothes and the dullness
of going to church on Sunday, there is not something
worth taking trouble about, possibly even a supremely
valuable thing, a pearl of great price. I expect it has
occurred to you, however, that in these very extraordinary times we have got a peculiarly good opportunity of making something of our supposed Christianity. Even we who have had as yet no great or
terrible war experience can say this—that ever since
we enlisted we have been living not for our own private
ambitions or amusements alone, and also that we have
undertaken and are even rather anxious to risk our lives.

This does us no particular credit. We really had no choice about joining. The fact remains, however, that in those two ways we are nearer than we used to be to Christ's situation in life, and this undoubtedly makes religion easier to fit on to our lives than it was three years ago.

At any rate, I have found it very much easier to take an interest in the subject, and this interest has proved of so much value that I am proposing to you to share it with me.

To avoid any misunderstanding, I had better say—First, that I have no idea what your attitudes may be towards this subject—and I am equally prepared to find you much farther advanced in it than I, or on the other hand, altogether disrespectful towards the whole business. Secondly, I have no wish to convert anybody to any belief. My object in reading this paper is really to satisfy the wish that always goes with a keen interest—namely, the wish to share it with other people.

Although, as I say, the war makes it easier to fit an interest in spiritual things into our lives, there are two objections to so doing, which I think men may still feel, and about which I propose to say a word.

We have a feeling that if we are going to try and get something, in the way of help or strength, or whatever it may be, out of the religion of Christ, we must give up our sins of the flesh, and lead very different lives. It is quite true that these sins are the exact opposite of the things of the Spirit, and that a man cannot have it both ways. There is nothing more disgusting than pious lechery. But it is very easy to make some such idea as this an excuse for neglecting the highest thing in our natures. We say : At any rate let us be honest brutes if brutes we are going to be—and although by putting it in that way we show that we care for something besides mere brutishness, we are content to leave that something undeveloped until our habits are confirmed, and it is almost impossible to change them.

Now to say, " I must be ' good ' "—whatever that means—"before I bother about Christ," is really very absurd. In fact, it is like putting the cart before the horse. You cannot know what good is until you bother about Christ. Then you will probably find it is something very different from what you thought. It is not the misdeeds of yesterday, but the intention to do the same to-morrow, that cannot be combined with an honest search for spiritual strength. But if a man, when not actually being tempted to the sins of the flesh, can say, " I hope I may not be tempted again," or, " I wish I were free from this weakness," then he is just the very man whom Christ said he was most willing to help. There can be no doubt that He very much preferred the society of sinners to that of the religious and pious people of His day.

Another objection which, under present circumstances, naturally arises is this : We got on very well without paying any attention to spiritual things before, and it is only a sort of cowardice to turn to them now. Were we really getting on very well before the war ? Certainly vast numbers were bitterly dissatisfied. Rich people were finding it harder and harder to get satisfaction from amusing themselves. Poor people were growing more and more impatient of dreary work, and dingy homes, and the general dullness of existence. Between these extremes those who were better off struggled to compete with the rich, those who were less well off dreaded falling to poverty. The war caught us when we were still young, and on the whole enjoying ourselves, but if we try and remember what we were like and what we were doing before war broke out, do we find that we had much to look forward to in a world which for the most part left God out of account ?

It is my own decided opinion that, in spite of all
its sorrows, the war, which, as I said at the beginning of
this paper, has forced us into something slightly resembling the position of Christ towards life, has, for
the time being at all events, made our lives less stupid
and ugly and small, more interesting in some ways,
and more satisfying to a proper pride in ourselves.
Should we want to go back to our old lives just as
they were? We cannot, of course, do so. The war
has changed them for good and all. But I see no
reason why, if we survive, we should not find that we
are sliding back into something nearly as uninspiring,
and probably much less prosperous. I think we shall need
God then—or at least something we hadn't got before.

Meanwhile you and I have not been out to France.
How are we going to cope with that? It is quite
certain that we want to do well there, to come out of
that test of our manhood without shame. Can it be
called cowardice to try and get hold of anything which
may help us, then? Rather, it is absolute folly to
neglect any means in our power of preparing ourselves for such an ordeal as we are now fast approaching. Nobody questions the need for military training
on the technical side. Nobody doubts either that
it is the spirit of armies, or regiments, or machine gun
teams, which in the end decides battles. If we are
to make a job of this show, no matter how well we
were getting on before the war, we need all we can get
of the great gifts of the spirit—calm and cheerfulness,
comradeship and courage.

The two objections, then, which I mentioned do
not, on inspection, prove to be fatal. There is really
no reason why we should not start on the search for
the Power of God. But the question now arises,
" Is there any such power? " It is easy to talk of
religion and spiritual life and God's help—the sort of
thing we have heard in church from our youth up—

but is there any substantial truth in it all ? The points we ought to satisfy ourselves about are—

First—Is there a spring of power, useful for everyday life in this world, which we could draw from, but which hitherto we have been content to neglect ?

Second.—Is this power, if it exists, the sort of thing we want ?

Third.—If it exists, and we want it, how are we to get it ?

The age of Queen Victoria, or the nineteenth century, was one of the most remarkable in the history of the world. The whole face of Western Europe, and indeed of the greater part of the world, has been changed by the discoveries of those times. The use of steam and the manufacture of steel, the discovery and development of electricity, are only the most obvious of the tremendous strides which men have recently made in their mastery of the world around them. Now that we can fly in the air and remain under the water, it seems as if the conquest of the visible world were complete. But if all our new knowledge and power has led to this war, the greatest and weariest slaughter ever known, it almost seems a doubtful question whether it was worth having.

Meantime, in all ages there have been men who believed in another field of knowledge and power, and sought a mastery over the invisible world, of thought, motive, will, and the like. This side of life is receiving just lately very much more attention than it did, say, ten years ago. You all probably know something about Christian Science. There are any number of faith-healing bodies coming into existence. America is the special home of these, but in this country too a movement away from material to immaterial objects of knowledge is very conspicuous. As we so often find, Christ was the Person who expressed this point most clearly. When He talked by the well with the woman of Samaria, He said: "If thou knewest the Gift of God and who it is that saith to thee, Give me to drink; thou wouldst have asked of Him and He would have given thee living water" (St. John 4).

I think it is quite certain that every man has in the deepest part of his nature that gift of God—that is to say, he is able to get hold of, and use as if it were his own, a power which he feels is not himself, but part of a much bigger and stronger Being. Most of us guess, and some are quite sure, that this power we dimly feel within us is the very same power that makes the world go round. If you attend honestly to the familiar facts about your own nature, you will come to the remarkable conclusion that, whether you like it or not, there was born in you not only a man, but also God.

There have always been men to whom some such knowledge as this has been the most important thing in life. They have felt that they were in the hands of a power which made their own private selves seem a trifling matter, and which provided the real motive force in their life, and at the same time a great personal uplifting in the other being's strength, a sense of being conquerors, triumphant masters of the world. St. Paul is a splendid example (2 Cor. ii 24–27, and Rom. viii 37).

The second question proposed was—Is this power the sort of thing we want? It would appear to vary very much in its effect upon different lives. The backbone of the thing, however, seems always to be the same—namely, the power to make a fresh valuation of the different facts of our experience, and also the power to take the consequences of so doing. When a man begins to explore this side of his nature—that which binds him to the unseen world of spiritual forces—he finds that a good many things he used to care a great deal about have become relatively unimportant, because of the greater importance of the new things he is discovering. Perhaps he was very anxious that people should think well of him—susceptible to the opinion of others. If he gets hold of the Gift of God he will not only know that he need not worry about his neighbours' idea of him, but he will actually be comparatively indifferent to it. Pleasures or indulgences which we have cherished will probably cease to occupy our minds, and we may find some difficulty in accounting for this to our old companions. We need to count the cost. But the result of developing our spiritual side ought to be that we shall be well physically, cheerful, generously minded to each other, fearless and confident. Now, if there is any chance of getting rid to some extent of illness, grumbling, selfishness, and funk, through the development of our spiritual powers, then surely this power is the thing above all others we most want.

Finally, how is such a power to be got ? Like everything else, it is to be had if we really want it. In this life we get, on the whole, what we make up our minds we want. The trouble is we want such stupid things, that we are not satisfied when we get them. In the first place, then, we must look ourselves fairly in the face, and we shall surely say : " I lack a lot—I am not always well, and I am often disagreeable, selfish, and afraid." This must be put a stop to as far as possible.

The next perfectly obvious step is to study the life and character of Jesus Christ. Many people seeking for the key to life, and spiritual power, leave out this step. This is quite clearly a great mistake. He was the most wonderful Person we know anything about, and merely being interested in Him and His story makes an immense difference to us. Do you remember what happened to Zacchæus ? (St. Luke xix. 1-10).

There are very puzzling passages in the New Testament, but it is clear that Christ Himself was—

First.—Well in health. He slept in the storm; and

over natural forces, and disease in others, He showed a power which must have extended to His own bodily health. There is not the smallest hint of disease reaching Him in the Gospels.

Second.—Cheerful. He went to marriage feasts. The pious people of His day said He was gluttonous and a wine-bibber. He was extraordinarily free from worry. He claimed to be the Son of God, and to have a unique message for the world. But He was quite content to have only a dozen followers, one of whom betrayed Him, and the rest deserted Him when His enemies got hold of Him. When He saw that all this was going to happen, He still could say, " Be of good cheer ; I have overcome the world."

Third.—Generous. He had powers of healing quite unlike any before or since, and He was always ready to use them for anybody who came and asked Him to do so.

Fourth.—He was brave and undismayed above all heroes.

The utmost injustice, stupidity, and cruelty, could not even ruffle Him for a moment, or turn Him from His sublime purpose of teaching men, not only how to live, but how to die.

In spite of all the dullness and unreality which is sometimes offered to us as His religion, we cannot help feeling that to appreciate the greatness of His character is beyond the power of our common speech. For while He was man, He was, in a supreme degree, man living in God, and God revealed in man.

It is possible for us to a limited extent to take Christ as our model. In the case of an ordinary friend or acquaintance whom we admire, we tend to grow like him in character. The more striking his character, the more he draws us after him. The unique character of Christ, even at this great distance of time, is the most stirring call to our spiritual natures, because we

169

can faintly realise the fact that His power, His wisdom, His character, were the very same as those which now and always give life and meaning to the whole world.

Before you go from here to Uckfield, and so to France, I have wanted to give to you, who have been those whom I have most enjoyed teaching in certain military matters, my thoughts on even more important things. I hope we shall meet again before long, if you would like it, and carry farther the beginning made to-night.

II

The last time we met we came to certain conclusions, and agreed to try and carry farther the beginning then made.

These conclusions were—(1) that it is a sensible thing to take account deliberately of the forces of an unseen world, to which many great men in all ages have attached the greatest importance; (2) that in this side of life there is a source of power, which might be made much more freely available than it is, for the concerns of our everyday life; and (3) that to get hold of this power, we have to realise that we stand in real need of something of this kind, while the next step is to increase our knowledge of Jesus Christ.

We might possibly hit on some way of taking this step together before long, but before considering that matter I think it would be better to discuss the practice universal among those who have lived in close relation with the invisible world, the practice of Prayer.

All Christians are supposed to pray; most children are taught to say their prayers; but as the children become men, a great many find that the practice is quite out of keeping with the rest of their lives, and give it up. Prayers are one of the principal parts of services in church, but they are somebody else's prayers, and are too often expressed in a peculiar set of general phrases, which mean little or nothing to us. In spite of this we may, I think, be quite sure that there is something in it. So many great men have found prayer to be the best way of drawing upon the Gift of God within them, that we cannot afford to neglect an effort to understand what prayer is, how we can use it, and what value it may have for us.

" Seize hold of God's hand, look full in the face of His creation, and there is nothing He will not enable you to achieve" (*Ruskin*).

We cannot do better than start with an example. At the Battle of Edge Hill, fought in 1640 between the royalist supporters of Charles I and the Parliament men, afterwards led by Cromwell, the King's standard was carried by Sir Edmund Verney. Before he went into the fight he prayed : " Lord, Thou knowest how busy I must be this day. If I forget Thee, do not Thou forget me, O Merciful Guardian." That is a prayer worth saying. We admire it because it is honest. There is no shutting of one eye to the things of common life about such a prayer as that. It is not only honest, but inspiring. It is a splendid confidence that takes it for granted that the connection between the visible and the invisible world is not a thing which concerns us on Sundays only, or in church, but all day and every day.

If we could pray like that it would be worth doing. Why can't we ? The chief reasons I think are : First, that while prayer is addressed to God, we don't know what we mean by God. If there is a God, we are more or less unfamiliar with Him. Second, that, whether because God does not exist, or does not care, or because we are not good enough, we think it would make little or no difference if we did pray. Prayer is usually explained, by those who use and value it, as speaking to God. But one feels it is ridiculous to talk to a Person of whom one has no clear idea at all. It is also certain that a great many things which really good people ask for in their prayers do not happen.

It seems, therefore, that, in order to understand what prayer may be for us, we must try and form some idea of God, and also ask ourselves in what sense we expect, or can reasonably hope, that our prayers will be answered.

Fully to understand God, to get a complete idea of Him, is impossible in this life. But that need not make us give up the attempt to form some idea of Him, which, though not complete, may be true, useful, and even satisfying.

It is really impossible to form a complete idea of another human being, but that does not prevent us from understanding our friends well enough to love them and to rely on them. Besides, when we try to enter into the meaning and power of the invisible world, it is not like starting to learn the mechanism of a maxim gun.

Whichever way we look at it, we are face to face with a mystery, we are setting out on a voyage of discovery. Where it may end we cannot tell, and we hardly want to know. The whole thing is an adventure.

I want to put two thoughts about God before you, which I believe to be true, and which to my mind are necessary to the right understanding of prayer.

In nearly all our prayers, including that of Sir E. Verney at Edge Hill, it is assumed that God is a Person altogether separate from us, who looks after us from outside, as a man might look after his horse on a day's march. Now, although it is quite certain that all those who have had true spiritual power have thought of God as infinitely greater than themselves, yet there is a sense, as we saw last time, in which God is actually to be found in each one of us. Christ Himself seems to have believed this. He says, " I am in the Father and the Father in me," and, "I and my Father are one." We cannot put it so strongly as that. The imperfection of our whole nature forbids us utterly to claim such a complete union with God; but still, I think we can say of God, first, that He is something very near to us—in fact the best part of ourselves; and, second, that through this fact we are connected up with the God " Who made heaven and earth, the sea, and all that in them is."

So we have two ideas of God, as we might have two ideas of another human being. It is He in us that makes our hearts sing sometimes, and our courage rise, and all the world seem our friend. That in us is God. Again, when we are carried out of our common round of interests and efforts, and forget our private selves altogether in the thought of a greater world than the one we usually call our own, the world where some mighty plan brings the sun up every morning, and rolls the earth at night through the wonderful system of the stars, then it is that we know that, being part of that world, we are in God's hands, that our true life is in Him.

We must think, then, of God in us, and also of ourselves in God, and so get an idea of what God is. The Lord's Prayer begins : " Our Father which art in Heaven." God is very near to us, and also very far above us, a very homely and also a very mysterious fact.

Now, when we pray to God we should pray to Him in both these ideas of Him, and when we have begun to think such thoughts of God we shall find that we have already begun to pray.

But in prayer we have an object. We pray for something we want, and the question we have asked ourselves is this : Are we likely to get it ?

When we speak of asking God for something, it is really to the God in us that we are praying. We are speaking to our own best selves, and forming the wish that the power of God within us should produce such and such results. We may ask for various kinds of results. They may depend principally on ourselves, principally upon other people, or principally on external things, such as the weather. For example, we might pray for cheerfulness; or for peace of mind. We might pray for leave to be granted us to go to Edinburgh, or, again, for fine weather on a field-day.

Now, so far as the matter depends upon ourselves, there can be no doubt that prayer is answered, or, rather, answers itself. By reminding ourselves deliberately of what we are trying to make of our own characters, we help ourselves, very powerfully, to succeed. The Psalms say: "Commune with thine own heart and in thy chamber, and be still." The value of some such moment of attention to the best that is in us, it is quite impossible to exaggerate. And this is truly to pray, if we believe that the best that is in us is God.

So far as the thing we ask in prayer depends upon other people, we have to remember that it is obviously not the plan upon which the universe is ordered, that one man can be forced to treat another well. It is absurd to think that God can force another man to give us leave to go to Edinburgh. The example of Christ helps us again. If God would not compel men to treat Him well, He certainly won't do more for us. The reason is that, as we have seen, there is God to be found in every man, so that it is ridiculous to suppose that the God who rules the heavens can compel, or overpower, a man on earth in whom He dwells. That would be treating Himself like a piece of machinery. But the point to bear in mind about such prayers as depend upon other men for their answers is, that prayer ought to be made in common. Men ought to pray together, and in the presence of God to make known to one another the things which they seek from one another. But even without prayer in common, it is, all the same, a good thing to pray for the things which depend on others for their coming to us. We do need such things constantly, and by remembering them before God, we can better control our aims, strengthen our purpose, and understand the right relation of our own to other men's lives.

So far as the things we seek depend on the external world around us—for example, on the weather—we do not at first sight seem to have much chance of getting them. But we must remember that we are on a voyage of discovery. We must not make up our minds that we shall never reach a certain country which now seems a very long way off. Two other points are worth making. The extent of the mastery of mind over matter is quite uncertain. In the power of taming the animals its beginnings go back beyond the memory of our race. In recent years, by mechanical means and scientific knowledge, we have gone forward in a marvellous way. Who can tell what may be the powers lying unused in our spiritual nature? We are only lately started in the investigation of these—that is to say, in an intelligent and sincere investigation. It is also impossible for Christians to forget that their whole religion, as a plain matter of history, rests on the fact that Christ rose from the dead. Nothing else can explain the existence of the Christian religion. It was this fact which turned the Apostles from doubtful followers, of very doubtful courage and reliability, into the men who founded the Christian Church, and for Christ's sake lived, worked, and died as martyrs.

Not only in His resurrection, but throughout His life, Christ showed Himself to be the Master of the external world. His healing of sick people was wonderful enough, and we have also the story of His stilling the storm, so that men were amazed at Him, and said, " What manner of man is this that even the winds and the sea obey Him ? " I think, therefore, that there is no reason why we should abstain from laying before God those needs of our daily life which depend for their satisfaction upon a power to control the world of nature.

There are many other kinds of prayer which we have not time to speak of to-night, such as the prayer for health, which depends for its answer partly upon ourselves, partly on other men, partly on external conditions, and the prayer for other people, which is called intercession, and which has always been thought to be natural and right. There are also the common experiences of feeling sorry for our wrong-doings, and thankful for our blessings, which also enter into prayer. But it is natural to begin with the expression of our own needs in prayer, and we may be content to go no farther in our present discussion.

There is one more side of prayer, however, which always comes in, and of which we must say something.

Up to now we have been thinking of that sort of prayer which is addressed to that within ourselves which is God. Its object is to develop the gift of God which is in us. In this way we may almost be said to be speaking to ourselves when we pray. But there is the other side of prayer which thinks of God as something going far beyond us, and when we think of this our private needs and efforts seem quite small and insignificant. This is really the greatest side of prayer, when our hearts and minds are lifted up above our everyday life into a bigger world. We remember then that we came into this world from we know not where, and that one day we shall pass out of life as mysteriously as we came into it. We realise then that we are in God's hands, and that it is enough for us to leave our lives, and the lives of those we love in His Almighty keeping. This side of prayer always brings its own answer. We come back to our own little world from the glimpse of that greater world, with what we may, perhaps, call more independence of mind. We shall worry less, we shall fear nothing, if we carry in our hearts the thought that we are in God, that in His care we live and move and have our being.

Now we have seen to a small extent the way we should look for our prayers to be answered. We have also formed some idea of God—the two thoughts, that is to say, of God in us and we in Him.

I am afraid that what I have written may appear altogether too complicated, and that if we have to think of all these things we shall never get started with prayer at all. That is quite true, but it is a good thing to try and think things out sometimes, so as to satisfy ourselves that we are not just taking somebody else's ideas at second-hand, and going in for some sort of trickery which won't bear too much examination, and is really rather nonsense at bottom. But prayer in practice is perfectly simple and easy, and the more simple and natural we make it, the better it is, and the more likely to find its answer.

You remember that when Christ was dying on the Cross, one of the thieves who were crucified with Him grumbled at His not being able to save them from so cruel and painful a death. But the other one somehow or other knew Who it was that was hanging beside him, and just said to Christ: " Lord, remember me when Thou comest into Thy Kingdom." That is a prayer we could all say, and Jesus answered and said to him: " Verily, verily, I say unto thee: this day thou shalt be with Me in Paradise."

That is really the whole truth about prayer—the more plainly and honestly we speak to God, the nearer we get to Him. We can hardly doubt which of the

N   177

two thieves died the more bravely. If we can make it our practice to turn our thoughts towards God every day we live, just when we have opportunity, and feel the need of Him, we shall go through the world braver, stronger, happier men.

Some of the shortest and most simple prayers are the very best; and, though it is in our own words that we should mostly pray, I should like to give you the prayer which comes from the English Confirmation Service—sometimes you may wish to use it:

" Defend, O Lord, these Thy children with Thy Heavenly Grace, that they may continue Thine for ever, and daily increase in Thy Holy Spirit more and more, until they come to Thine Everlasting Kingdom."

III

In our first two papers we sought to satisfy ourselves that the life of the Spirit was a genuine, possible and valuable thing, and that prayer, which has been of so much importance to great men in the past, was for us, also, the best way of entering into the invisible world, and drawing from it the power we need for our everyday life.

We found that, in attempting to develop and improve our spiritual nature, we were brought face to face with forces we could not estimate, and mysteries we could not fathom—" the deep things of God," as St. Paul calls them—so that we described the attempt to live this highest kind of life as a voyage of discovery. Once we have embarked on the adventure, our part is largely that of faith—the conviction, that is, that though with man many things seem impossible, yet with God all things are possible. He, who is the Port in which we hope to end our journey, is Himself also the only means whereby we can reach it. Trust in God's power and protection, God's faithfulness, and

God's love will see us through, if we keep our hearts and minds set upon the great purpose of our adventure. For, " no man having set his hand to the plough and looking back is fit for the Kingdom of God."

Happily for us, therefore, the spiritual life is not a voyage across a sea, forlorn and deserted, towards a country still unseen beyond the horizon. It is better compared to the climbing of a hill, when, as we go up, the range of our view grows gradually wider. When we reach the top there will, we believe, be a new and glorious country laid out before us; but even as we climb the lower slopes we expand and enrich our knowledge of the land from which we set out. For this too, when from the crest we can take it all in, will form part, with the unknown land beyond, of the glorious heritage of the sons of God.

This increase and development of our spiritual range, as we ascend the hill of the Lord, is God's part in response to our venture of faith. As we grow in the power of trusting Him, so He reveals Himself more and more to us through Jesus Christ. God does not leave us to find our way to Him without a guide. " For God so loved the world that He gave His only-begotten Son that whosoever believeth on Him should not perish, but have everlasting life." To perish is to be shut out of God's Kingdom, but the life eternal, as St. John says, is that " we should know God, through Jesus Christ whom He has sent."

Hitherto we have thought of the life of the spirit as being a direct relation between man and God. This is at the bottom of all true religion. We seek nothing less than God Himself, and we believe that that which speaks to us, and uplifts us when we lift up our hearts and minds in prayer, is nothing less than God Himself. It is all-important to hold fast to this direct knowledge and experience of God, for without that foundation, other religious beliefs are only built upon the sand. But to help us to build securely upon that foundation, we have available the story and the teaching of Jesus Christ.

You will perhaps remember that in the first paper I said I thought one of the surest ways of laying hold of the forces of the invisible, or spiritual world, was to increase our knowledge of Jesus Christ. It is a great thing to be religious in a general way—to believe that there is a God, and that in prayer we can come into contact with Him; but it is an even better and stronger thing to be religious also in a special way, to be definitely a Christian, to believe that in the life and thought of Jesus Christ we have a true revelation of the character and purpose of Almighty God. The Christian religion exists to assert the truth of Christ's words when He said: " He that hath seen Me hath seen the Father . . . I and my Father are one."

Now, I don't wish to say that a man cannot lead a good life, and a spiritual life, without being a Christian; but I am satisfied for myself that it is easier to live well if we believe in the revelation of God to us in the life and death and resurrection of Christ, and I am sure, also, that we should do our best to get an idea of what that revelation was before we go in for Christian Science, or any other of the new ways of approaching God, and declare that Christianity is played out.

I propose, therefore, that in this and a succeeding paper, which I hope I shall be able to read before you go, that we should consider what it is which Christ tells us about God, and what sort of a pattern it is which He sets before us.

Christ reveals God to us in three principal ways: He reveals Him as Power, as Judgment, and as Redemption.

These are all ideas which want some thinking over before we understand them. We have, however, said a good deal already about the Power of God. It is the idea of God to which men are most attracted at the present time. We have thoroughly explored the regions of mechanical and scientific power, and still all is not well with us. We seek to bring into our lives the Power of God. It was so in our Lord's time, and in the early days of the Church which the Apostles founded. Men came from all parts to hear what Christ had to say, when they heard of the wonderful works which He performed, and it is quite clear, from the book of the Acts, that those who had been with Christ were able to show signs and wonders, and thereby to attract men's attention to their preaching. We are absolutely in accord, therefore, with the revelation of Christ, as it is contained in the Gospels and the Acts, in seeking to realise the Power of God, "both outwardly in our bodies and inwardly in our souls."

In this respect Christian Science and similar movements, which aim at bringing the power to heal by spiritual means back into our ordinary estimate of religious forces, are more faithful to Christ than the Christian Churches. If we want to follow Christ, we must see to it that we do not shut up our minds against the belief that, as shown by Him, God is willing to help us in all our troubles of whatever kind. If we do not see very clear evidence of God's Power in our daily lives, it is much more likely to be our fault than His. The more we get hold of this, the nearer we shall be to getting back to the more satisfying experiences of the Early Christians.

I will say no more on the subject of God's Power as revealed by Jesus Christ. God's work of Redemption—that is, of bringing us into union with Himself—I will try and say something about in another paper. There remains the revelation by Christ of God as Judgment. What do I mean by that?

It is not true that Christ shows us the character of God as an angry, vindictive Person, condemning human beings to roast in hell fire.

Christ Himself lived a perfect life, perfectly good in the ordinary sense of the word, and perfectly centred upon God. With Him every joy would have been a thanksgiving, every trouble an acceptance of God's Will. In contrast with His perfection He shows us clearly, what is bad, and what it is which keeps us away from God. We mentioned the other night the possibility of a man keeping up his habit of prayer openly in billets. Such a man's action would be a judgment on all of us for our slackness and feebleness of faith. So it is with the Judgment of God, as revealed by Christ. His life shows us what to aim at in life, and what to avoid. He gives His verdict upon life. I believe that, if we reject His verdict, the punishment follows automatically. But that is our affair. Now, what is that verdict?

It is a stern one in many ways. There is no getting out of that. They who would follow Christ have got to march up-hill, not down. After all, it is no more than common sense that life is not a go-as-you-please affair. If we have any object whatever in view, we know perfectly that it does matter what we do and what we leave undone. In the highest things of life this is especially true, and I think if we are honest we shall be glad of this, and welcome the need to pull ourselves together, to make up our minds about what is good and evil, and to stick it out like men.

The parable of the Sower is a passage which shows us very clearly what Christ taught about the verdict which God pronounces upon our lives (St. Mark iv).

There are the three classes of people from whom God reaps no harvest of strong and joyful lives:

First, the people whose hearts are like the hard, trodden wayside path. The word or message of God

makes no impression on them at all. It lies on the
surface for a moment, as they hear the truth with
their physical ears, and immediately the birds come
and pick it up, and it might just as well never have
been brought before them. What sort of people are
these? Those on whom Christ Himself could make
no impression, even the Scribes and Pharisees, so the
Gospels tell us. Christ called them hypocrites, and
was grieved for the hardness of their hearts. Can
we say of ourselves that we are in no way like them?
I am afraid we often have a seed of God's Word sown
for us, and it bounces off, so that we go on in our everyday lives just the same as before. If this were not
so, our public and general life in the world would be
very different from what it is. We find it very hard to
allow God's Word a say all through the day. How
much of God's Word and message do we bring on
parade, and how much of it do we remember in the
mess-hut and in billets? We are all more or less hard-
hearted. Why is it? Christ called the hard-hearted
of His day hypocrites. The word means "actors,"
and I think that word gives us the key with which we
can unlock our hearts and let God in. We are actors
too. We have some idea of our own about ourselves
which we are trying to realise, just as an actor tries
to represent his part. We have never bothered to ask
whether this part we propose to ourselves to play is
the part God intended for us, the part which is really
our own, because it agrees with the gift of God within
us. There are any number of such parts which we
commonly act. For example, we go in for being a
man of the world, making his way boldly through
life, not too squeamish about right and wrong, reflect-
ing that, if a man doesn't look out for himself, nobody
else is going to look out for him. Again, we may go
in for being a sportsman, a jolly sort of fellow who
doesn't care a damn what happens. Or we may set

before ourselves the idea of simply having a good time, or, again, of being generally respected and looked up to as a successful man by all our acquaintances and neighbours. We accept these pictures of ourselves, these parts we propose to play, like actors on a stage, without thinking much about them, and they become so habitual that any suggestion which does not fit in with them simply bounces off us, leaving no impression at all. What has Christ to say about all this? Two things, I think. First, these ideas are idols; they are our false Gods. Christ says: pull them down, knock them off their pedestals. There is only one God, and Him only shalt thou serve. Second, when you have knocked them down to their proper levels, bring them before me, compare them with my plan of life, and you will see how much in them is good and how much is bad.

I do not attribute this judgment of our little aims and ideals to Christ without being able to show from the Gospels that He did give such a verdict. Take the case of the man of the world (St. Luke xvi 1–8). Though the unjust steward's cleverness was actually commended, nevertheless his master does not change the decision. " Thou mayest be no longer steward."

The story of the Prodigal Son illustrates Christ's attitude towards a reckless, though amiable, character. A complete change of mind is necessary to bring him back into his father's home, and restore him to his father's love. The same parable shows how little Christ cared for respectability if it stands in the way of a man's love for his fellow-man (Luke xv 2).

In what Christ said to Simon the Pharisee (Luke vii 36), and the parable of the Good Samaritan, we can see very plainly what He thought of any superiority of education, social position, or of religious observance, when it did not prevent a want of tenderness for the sins and sorrows of other men and women. It is equally plain that He bids us compare our ideas of ourselves with His own conduct and character. He says, " I am the Way, the Truth and the Life "; " No man cometh to the Father but by Me "; " I am the Good Shepherd "—our best guide; " I am the true Vine "—the stock from which we should draw our principle of life. He offers Himself to us as a touch-stone with which we can test our standard, and distinguish the true and eternal from the false and mean ideals of human life, thought, and action.

There is one point in which we are very apt to feel quite sure we are right, and that is when we stick out for our rights, and refuse to be put upon. Christ has not much use for that rather favourite attitude of ours. " But I say unto you, Love your enemies, bless them that curse you, do good to them that hate you " (Matt. v 44).

This seems very extreme, very difficult. Christ does not deny that. " Strait (meaning small) is the gate, and narrow is the way which leadeth unto life, and few there be that find it "; but He claims unhesitatingly that His view is not fantastical, but simply common sense (Matt. vii 24). (He practised what He preached.) Such, then, is Christ's judgment upon our common ideas about ourselves. They form a sort of crust or shell of hardness round our hearts. We need to break this up before the Word of God can take root within us.

The second class of people alluded to in the parable of the Sower are the faint-hearted. Though they start well, they soon collapse, and bring in nothing at harvest-time. They cannot endure any " afflic-tion " for the Word's sake.

People are not much persecuted in our time for their religious opinions or practices. They may be laughed at sometimes, but on the whole I doubt whether it can be said that other men make it seriously more difficult for us to follow Christ. Our faint-heartedness more often comes out in the thinness and poorness of our own belief. We don't care keenly enough about making the best of life. We are content to be second-class shots. This was more true before the war than it is now. Our meeting as we have done lately, to talk over these things, shows that just at present, owing to the unusual position in which we find ourselves, we are able to receive the Message of God.

Whether or no the Word has fallen in our case upon poor ground, where there is not much depth of earth, will be better seen after the war, if we come back to our ordinary civilian occupations.

People to whom Christ appealed, when He was on earth, felt the same fear that the seed would be withered before harvest. The Disciples said to him : " Increase our faith," and another declared : " Lord, I believe ; help Thou mine unbelief."

The Apostles had to wait till after Christ was crucified and risen again, and then for a further period, until something happened, which is called the coming of the Holy Ghost, to transform their unbelief into so powerful a conviction that through them the whole course of history was altered.

We shall probably have to show patience—it was one of Christ's most striking qualities—but two things we can do to increase our faith. First, we can give ourselves the trouble to find out, in a simple and ordinary way, about the facts of religious experience in ourselves, and the revelation of God made by Jesus Christ.

Second, we can practise ourselves in the art (one may almost call it so) of connecting our thoughts about the highest things with the incidents of our common life. It may seem difficult, or silly, or even irreverent, to connect the thought of God with platoon drill; but I cannot see myself how, if we are in God and He in us, the thought of Him can be incongruous with any honest activity or harmless pleasure.

We may know our drill well, and feel contemptuously irritated with those who cannot remember which is left and which right. We may be doing it badly, and feel thoroughly fed-up. We may be getting through it passably, but feeling bored to death by it. In each case we are allowing ourselves to get into a frame of mind which is not only bad in itself, but demoralising.

Evil is not merely the doing of positively wicked things, but also the not doing of good things, and the not feeling vigorous and cheerful and kindly. We can serve God, and increase our ability to serve Him, by remembering and trying to act upon this idea. Is it not extraordinarily foolish to do anything else? Who was ever the least bit the better for being bored or disagreeable? Everyone who is vigorous, cheerful, and kindly, is God's servant, whether he knows it or not. But if he does know it he will be able to increase these good qualities in himself, to deepen and enrich the soil of his character, and in the end to hear the imperishable welcome of his Master: " Well done, thou good and faithful servant."

The third class of persons who bring no fruit to perfection are those in whom the seed springs up into blade, but is choked by the weeds, which are the trumpery cares and concerns of everyday life.

You remember the story of Martha and Mary? (Luke x 38). I do not think that Christ means that we are to let common duties and routine work go undone, or be done in a slovenly way. He calls us to a sense of proportion, and tells us to care most for those things which are most worth caring for. It is only common sense, once more, to say: Don't fuss or worry. As far as you possibly can, keep your head above the drowning waters of anxiety. Christ tells us that our Heavenly Father knows very well that we have need of the ordinary things of life. To earn our living is a necessity, but He says : " Seek ye first the Kingdom of God and His righteousness, and all these things shall be added unto you." Don't forget to be like Mary, because Martha was very likely a most capable and worthy housekeeper. She would have been a better one still if she had been less cumbered by her duties, for she would have given an even better welcome to that Guest whom she most wished to honour. Men, and especially when soldiering, are to a great extent free from the smallest worries, which are the ones hardest to be rid of, if we have them ; but small, trivial, and really very ridiculous things do often pester our lives, and leave us no time to let God's Word grow up in our hearts.

Such it seems is God's Judgment, on our lives and characters, as revealed in the life and teaching of Jesus Christ.

It is revealed above all in the facts of His life and character. It is His greatness which displays our littleness, and His greatness consists in the fact that He " came not to be ministered unto, but to minister, and to give His life a ransom for many."

This brings us to the thought of Christ's revelation of the redemption of God. I will try and show in another paper how and why it is that we speak of Christ as our Saviour.

IV

In the current number of a weekly paper called *The Challenge* the following words are printed: " It is probable that the deepest impulse moving in religion is the desire for friendly intercourse with a power

<hr>

[1] In a late letter (p. 66) he identified " Judgment " with discernment.

capable of giving help and protection, and willing to do so."

This sentence summarises the thoughts of our first two papers. In the third we went on to consider the revelation of God in Christ which is available to meet this impulse. We found that this revelation carried us beyond the rather vague sense, with which religion begins, of the presence of a great and friendly though unseen power, to an understanding of the character and purpose of God.

It appeared that we were in accord with the life and teaching of Jesus Christ in seeking the Power of God to give us health and happiness, " both outwardly in our bodies, and inwardly in our souls." We then considered the judgment, or verdict, which by the greatness of His character, expressed both in thought and action, Christ gives upon our standards of conduct, and our aims in life. A knowledge of His mind gives us a sharp, and in some ways a surprising, line of division between what we do well to follow, and what we do well to avoid. On the one side of this line are selfishness or hardness of heart, feebleness of faith, and concentration upon the small or base interests of our lives. We did not develop to any extent the qualities which stand on the other side of the line. It is plain, however, that they are—openness of heart, forgetfulness of self, and ready sympathy with others, determination to trust God out and out, right through the common course of each day, and a continual lifting of our minds towards the highest notion we can approach of the grand possibilities of a human soul in this world and the world to come.

It is very important, however, to remember that the object with which Christ came into the world was to show us a God whose plan it was not to judge the world of men, but to save, or help, or redeem mankind, by bringing it into union with Himself.

" For Christ came not into the world to condemn the world, but that the world through Him might be saved."

The judgment, or separation of good from evil, is closely connected with the purpose of redemption, because God has allowed to men, alone of His creatures, the possibility of taking an active part with Him in the accomplishment of His plan. He therefore shows us what is good, and what evil; for good is that which brings us nearer to Him, and evil that which keeps us away from Him. We are, then, in a position to avoid the latter, and choose the former, and so help ourselves to become in the end united with Him, to take a full share in the Divine Nature. But, whatever we do, God's plan remains the same—to save.

God gave us life here on earth, and the wonderful gift of freedom—the chance, that is, to shape our own course through the world to a great extent. It is this gift which gives to our existence all its point and value, and which distinguishes us from the animals or the lifeless world of earth and sky and sea. But God does not leave us without a help to use this great chance of ours in the way which will bring about our real happiness. He is for ever saving us from the disaster of using it in the wrong way. He will not make us go the right and sensible way by force, for thus it would bring us no real happiness. His plan is finer than that, and requires a much higher sort of power. His plan is to win our hearts and minds to a genuine, independent love. of Himself, so that willing and joyfully we enter into His Heavenly Kingdom.

This wonderful work of God, His Divine Purpose of Redemption, was revealed to men in the life of Jesus Christ. The purpose did not begin with the coming of Christ, nor end with His death. It always has gone on, and always will go on. It was made plain to men, revealed by Christ. But in such a matter as this, to make the purpose plain is to go a great way towards realising and accomplishing it. By showing us God's love for us, He draws an answering love from our hearts. That is why Christ Himself is thought and spoken of as being in a special degree the Redeemer, or Saviour of the world.

We must go rather more carefully into the idea of Christ as the Saviour if we want to grasp it in such a way that it will really help us, and so prove itself true in our case.

When it is said that God, especially in Christ, was and is redeeming the world, we naturally ask—first, what is He redeeming us from; second, by what means is He working this redemption; and, third, into what condition does His redemption bring us?

From what, then, does Christ save us?

It used to be thought, and perhaps it is still believed, that when God was angry with men, and intended to destroy them, Jesus Christ, by the goodness of His life and the painfulness of His death, compensated for the sins of men, and, as it were, put God in a good temper again, or at any rate made it possible for God to give up His intention of sending every Jack man of us to hell.

It is ridiculous nonsense of this sort which consciously, or unconsciously, disgusts men with religion altogether. We entirely decline to accept such an idea of God as is suggested by the above. It is revolting in many ways. To take but one point, we can only worship a God who at any rate knows His own mind. It is quite impossible that Christ was turning God from His previous intention of destroying the world. He says Himself that He came to do His Father's will, and carry out His Father's plan. We altogether reject the notion, therefore, that Christ came to save us from the wrath or anger of God.

Christ does not save us from God, but from ourselves.

What is it that we are most hampered by ? What is it which keeps us bound like prisoners ? What is it that prevents our best nature from triumphing over our worse ? At bottom it is ignorance. As Jesus Christ said of the people of Jerusalem, we do not *know* the things that belong to our peace—the things which would make us really happy. We may even know them with our brains, but we are ignorant of them in our bones. We don't possess the sort of knowledge which enables us to act in such a way that we make the best of life, either as individuals or as a nation. We are ignorant of the principles which lie below the surface, and we can't get hold of the way in which the show is being run. We are ignorant of God. It is from this profound ignorance of ours that Christ can, and will, save us.

Now, without Christ it is hardly possible for us to know much about God. We have said that a personal experience, or sense of God, in our own hearts is the foundation of all real religion. This is to my mind absolutely true; but we need something to give more exactness to our ideas of God. This we have offered to us by Christ. He says, "He that hath seen Me hath seen the Father." It is our business to try and understand what Christ really was, and what He proposed that we should be, till we have such a knowledge of Him that the knowledge leads immediately to action, just as we " half load " when the gun stops with the crank handle vertical. Then, if we find that action based on this knowledge brings us greater power and happiness, brings us nearer to what every man longs for, and which the Gospels call the Kingdom of Heaven, then we shall see how true it is that Christ, by taking away our ignorance of God, has been our Saviour.

I shall mention briefly two points in respect of which Christ takes away our cramping ignorance of God. It is often said that Christ redeemed us from sin. What does this mean ? As early as St. Paul's time, who was born before Christ died, people were saying that by redeeming us from sin it was meant that when God had said, "Right turn!" and we had made a slovenly sort of turn to the left, Christ intervened and said it was no matter. It was thought that we were under an obligation to be moral—*e.g.*, not to lie—and that, though we did lie, Christ let us off the punishment which would otherwise have followed on our breaking the law of God ; and not only that, but that He also somehow made things " as you were "—as if we hadn't broken the rules at all.

All this is very much like the absurdity of thinking that Christ redeemed us from the wrath of God. Throughout His life on earth Christ was always protesting against this lawyer's view of right and wrong. He had · the greatest contempt for that notion of life which makes it a matter of Divine regulation and human obedience—rules made by God, and binding upon human beings. He is constantly warning His followers against the leaven of the Scribes and Pharisees. They were people who looked at life in this way, and, by using the word " leaven " of their ideas, He evidently meant that they were deceptively, insidiously evil—a regular trap into which we must take care not to fall.

Then, again, take His own death. There never was such a case of breaking the rules as that. He was perfectly good, and without any kind of excuse He was condemned to the most cruel and humiliating death. Nevertheless, He accepted this as God's will. Just think what that means. It was God's will that this outrageous thing should happen. After that we can hardly believe that God has imposed the rules. If He makes the rules and then wills that they should be flagrantly broken, He is not a God we can worship.

What, then, are good and evil, right and wrong, as

o   193

shown by the life and death of Christ? I do not
pretend for a moment to be able to give a complete
answer to this question, but I feel sure of this—that
right is what leads us to God, and wrong is what leads
us away from Him. God will not punish us if we
turn away from Him. He wants our love, not our
obedience. But punished we shall be, and terribly
indeed, if we deliberately reject the chance He has
given us of entering His Kingdom.

"There shall be weeping and gnashing of teeth"
—don't we see it now?—as Christ says, when we
find we have chosen the things which turn to dust and
ashes; and have shut ourselves off from God's Presence,
and cut ourselves out of the splendid inheritance
which was ours. "The wages of sin," says St. Paul,
"is death; but the gift of God eternal life."

Make no mistake about it, right and wrong are the
most important things in the world, far more tremendous in what depends upon them than any breaking or keeping of rules. Christ has shown us what
things are right, and what wrong, and He has shown us
what right and wrong really mean and involve for us.
Unless He drove us like sheep into His Kingdom, what
more could He do?

There can be no doubt how we shall choose, once
we know what He has done for us. If, then, you wish
to follow right, to take up your inheritance in Christ's
Kingdom, to enter into the joy of your Lord, never
think of right as a legal obligation, something which
you *ought* to do, but as something which with all your
heart you must love to do, because it is the condition
of your own happiness, progress, and power.

Never reject the redemption brought by Christ,
from the bondage of a law we could never satisfy, into
the freedom of brotherhood with Him who is the
Son of God.

Another point which Christ's life makes clear to us,

is the place of suffering in the world. He suffered to the utmost, morally and physically. His Divinely beautiful and tender nature was outraged and insulted with the worst of cruelty and stupidity. No one was ever so unjustly treated as He. His body, which He seems to have known how to keep in perfect health, and which He absolutely controlled by His Spirit, was tortured and destroyed in the most brutal form of public execution. What is the meaning of this? It is another revelation of God's character. In our ignorance we think that goodness will get us an earthly reward, that our virtues will be recognised in the end. If Christ truly shows us the nature of God, this idea is quite wrong. He showed that suffering itself was a Divine thing, and that God Himself could taste of death. We, therefore, are never to run away from injustice or pain. We are not to be afraid of them any more. We may confidently risk the contempt of men, and the collapse of our bodily selves, because Christ has shown that the Divine element in us is altogether above these things, and that, in our times of greatest trial and distress, we may be coming nearer to God, and tasting more fully the strength of His power and protection. Here, again, Christ the Redeemer has shown us that we can be free from the bitterness of revolt against the hard things of life. It is possible for a man to take these blows full in the face without a word, and to come out stronger than ever in this life, or, if need be, " to depart and be with Christ, which is far better."

There is, indeed, abundance of meaning in the Redemption of our Lord Jesus Christ.

Our second question was—By what means is the Redemption carried out?

It was begun with the beginnings of human nature. For as soon as our natures could be called human, God began revealing Himself to men, and bringing them to a capacity for understanding Him. Then, by the coming into the world of Jesus Christ, the nature of God was declared, and ever since God the Holy Spirit has continued the work, which He began so many thousands of years ago, the work of developing and renewing our inner lives.

The life of Christ is the foundation, but the Temple of God to be built on it—that is to say, a world redeemed and brought into full harmony with God—that is not yet completed. Christ did not claim, when He was on earth, to have finished the whole purpose of God for mankind. He speaks of the Holy Spirit, the Comforter as He is called in the Gospels, who will carry on His work in the world, and of a day of triumph, the second coming of Christ, when the redemption of human nature shall be finally accomplished.

This thought, that the redemption of man by God is still going on, corresponds with our experience. We feel that as the woods and fields are for ever renewing themselves, so that God's *creation* still seems to be going on, so also in our own lives the Spiritual power is always capable of being renewed and refreshed, and our natures are constantly receiving new opportunities of drawing nearer to God. This is the *redeeming* work of the Holy Spirit.

Two points here seem to me clear and important:

First.—We must not allow ourselves to be despondent about our own spiritual progress. We are all liable to ups and downs. Very often we feel quite unable to get a practical grip of the truth we hold with our minds. It is quite possible to realise distinctly what we must do to inherit eternal life, but somehow to fail in setting about it. If we remember, then, that God is still redeeming the world from its ignorance of Him, we shall be able to watch and wait for the saving Word, which will give us the thought of God we are needing in order to get on the move once more in our journey up the mountain. God does, I think, explain Himself to us directly, and especially if we keep on the watch for His Message. Some thought may come into our minds, some incident may touch our hearts, so that we feel again the sense we had lost of God's presence in the world, of the happiness of seeking for Him, and of the joy of meeting Him.

Second.—If the Holy Spirit is redeeming the world still, He is redeeming it *through us.* Each one of us has, as we saw in our first paper, something of the Spirit of God within him. Something in us is God. Then, since God's work is that of helping, saving, and enlightening human nature, our work is the same. Each of us possesses this wonderful chance of sharing in the work of God.. We are all in our way redeemers. We none of us live alone, and our lives have more influence on each other than we always remember. We have the possibility of showing in our own lives more or less of the character of God, and of bringing the knowledge of Him to the help of others. At the same time we receive from others the same sustaining and uplifting message. We are all bound up with one another, and the happiness of each one of us depends, to a very great extent, upon the happiness of all.

To be truly happy is to know and love God, and when all men know and love Him, and not before, the Kingdom of Heaven will be come.

Remember this, then—that as you try and understand and seek to follow Christ by attending to the Word of God's Holy Spirit within you, and giving it room in your lives to soften and strengthen them, so you are sharing in the very life and work of Christ, whom His and our Heavenly Father sent into the world, that the world through Him might be saved.

This brings us to our third question: Into what condition does God's redemption bring us?

Christ always speaks of Himself as preaching the

Kingdom of God, and in various parables conveys to us what He understood that phrase to mean. It is to this Kingdom that Christ's work of redemption brings us.

A great deal of rubbish has been thought and written about Heaven, into which harps and golden crowns and hallelujahs are introduced with a strikingly depressing effect. I think, though the subject of Heaven must be difficult, that we can do better than that. I will try and put three thoughts before you:

First.—The Kingdom of Heaven is a society. Its social character is a most important point. Christ does not come to save us, and bring us into His Kingdom one by one, but all together.

Second.—This Kingdom consists of a spiritual condition in its members. It depends upon a change in their minds, a transformation of their estimate of and outlook on life, whether in this world or the next.

Third.—The motto and sole principle of this society is called Love. " A new commandment give I unto you that ye love one another." These are Christ's words, and they are the clue to His teaching about the Kingdom He came to found.

It begins in this world when men meet together for any purpose in a generous and sympathetic frame of mind, and honestly try to help, to understand, and to value one another. In any other life which may lie beyond the grave we may be perfectly sure that no selfish happiness will crown the efforts of those who have tried to lead unselfish lives on earth. Jesus Christ says : " Follow Me," and He means, I think, that to follow Him is not merely to be on the road to eternal life, but that following Him is the life eternal. No private advantage lies at the end of the journey, for following Christ means becoming more and more devoted, not to oneself, but to the work of offering one's strength of body, gifts of mind, powers of imagination or sympathy, and even one's bodily life, in the service of our fellow-men. We shall probably find that in so trying to follow Christ we shall be constantly experiencing, on a small scale as it were, His death and resurrection. We shall need to nerve our hearts to do difficult things, and to accept misunderstanding by others of what we are doing. Life, as we have said before, will be an adventure. But if, as St. Paul says, we have to die daily, there is no doubt, in the report of those who have so lived for Christ, that death is nothing but the gateway leading to life.

If we dare anything for His sake, in His power our soul's victory is certain. It is a grand call. There is a ring about it which wakes one's manhood. Christians in all times, who have deserved the name, have been a small company striking out into the unknown. They are pioneers always, pointing to things they cannot altogether explain, trusting in God for strength, for knowledge, and for the triumph of their faith.

Since we have been meeting here we must, I think, have felt that we had a little more idea than we had before of the meaning of the Kingdom of Heaven. Wherever men who honour one another meet to speak the truth, and to search out the secrets of God, there the Kingdom is come. We know that there is no happiness to compare with this, and that these hours have spread their influence over the rest of our lives, not only in relation to one another, but to other men. Now we are to be parted, or, rather, I am to be parted from you. I hope this will not be for long. But let us swear to remember, to cheer ourselves with the memory, wherever our ways may lead us, that we have tasted together the finest fruit of life, that we have had a glimpse in one another of the Kingdom of God.

" Let all anger and clamour and evil speaking be put away from you with all malice, and be ye kind one to another, tender-hearted, forgiving one another, even as God for Christ's sake hath forgiven you."

A PRAYER WRITTEN FOR THE MEN

ALMIGHTY GOD, who hast promised that when two or
three are gathered together in Thy name Thou art there
in the midst of them, help us to understand that Thou art near
to every one of us, and that Thou art able and willing to share
our joys and sorrows.

Standing in Thy presence, we tell Thee what things we need
in our daily lives. We need health and strength. We need
cheerfulness and courage. We need to be good comrades to
one another We need to remember more than we do the
example of Jesus Christ, and to remember how He thought of
others before Himself, and promised eternal life to all who try
and follow Him.

These and many other things we need. Lord, give us what
we need, and help us to be Thy faithful soldiers and servants
unto our life's end.

We believe that Thou dost help and cheer all that truly turn
to Thee. We entrust our lives to Thy holy keeping.

Defend, O Lord, us Thy children with Thy heavenly grace,
that we may continue Thine for ever ; and daily increase in
Thy Holy Spirit more and more, until we come to Thine
everlasting Kingdom.

February 1917.

Printed by Hazell, Watson & Viney, Ld , London and Aylesbury.

CPSIA information can be obtained at www.ICGtesting.com
Printed in the USA
LVOW112028200712

290934LV00012B/95/P